For Rent
By Owner

For Rent By Owner

Hassle-free Landlording from *A* to *Z*

Larry Prosser

BOB ADAMS, INC.
PUBLISHERS
Holbrook, Massachusetts

Published by Bob Adams, Inc.
260 Center Street, Holbrook, MA 02343

ISBN: 1-55850-251-3

Printed in the United States of America.

J I H G F E D C B A

This book is available at quantity discounts for bulk purchases. For information, call 1-800-872-5627.

This publication is designed to provide accurate and authoritative information with regard to the subject matter covered. It is sold with the understanding that the publisher is not engaged in rendering legal, accounting, or other professional advice. If legal advice or other expert assistance is required, the services of a competent professional person should be sought.

— From a *Declaration of Principles* jointly adopted
by a Committee of the American Bar Association and a
Committee of Publishers and Associations

The business of being a landlord is a complex one; the information in this book is meant as an observation of general trends and examples in this field, not as legal or professional advice for specific problems.

Cover design: Marshall Henrichs.

Foreword

For Rent By Owner is a straightforward, practical guideline of the complexities of managing rental income property.

No longer can an owner/investor casually undertake management. Whether the investment is small or large is irrelevant. The same laws, the same interpersonal skills, the same record keeping, and the same management techniques are required.

There is no substitute for "hands on" knowledge in any business. For many owners the first investment is the first experience with a rental property. It can develop into a maze of frustration and legal entanglements if the owner is not in some way guided in the right direction. Larry Prosser, through his own experience and hours of research spent with other owners and managers, has compiled a vast amount of information to make owning and managing a little easier. Owning rental property is a business, and the management of it will be the key as to whether the owner stays in business.

Professionals in the rental industry have long known that education is a must to being successful. Laws are changing constantly. From the initial contact with a resident, whether it be in person or on the telephone, it becomes critical that all aspects of renting are handled in a fair and unbiased manner. Using proper forms ensures equal protection for both the owner and the resident. Using good management practices will ensure the maximum success of the investment.

Among the tools of the trade are good reference books. As a manager of a trade association representing owners and managers of rental property, I recognize the value of having publications that can reinforce the verbal advice we offer to our members. *For Rent By Owner* allows the reader to understand step-by-step the practical aspects of management. Learning the hard way without a proper education is a painful and expensive process. No one can guarantee that problems will disappear with good management, but certainly they are minimized by good advice and that is what Larry's book is all about.

Betty Gwiazdon, CAE
Executive Vice President,
Sacramento Valley Apartment Association, Inc.

Contents

CHAPTER 1

Do You Really Want to Manage Your Own Rentals?

If you own your own home, you are already managing property. That realization is what lures many investors into the residential rental business in the first place. You keep tax records and prepare household budgets (more or less); you pay the mortgage, insurance, utilities, and repair bills. You probably even do some or most of your home repairs. So what's the difference between doing it for your own home and doing it for a house you rent to someone else? The difference is that someone else!

That someone else (a.k.a. THE TENANT) transforms that house into a business. Owning and managing residential rentals is a business venture that requires using certain business skills, people skills, and investment skills. It is a people business, subject to some very tricky laws, and requiring specific knowledge about the business. And some very understanding attitudes and behavior on the part of the owner/manager.

During one of the first property management courses I took, the instructor stressed that managing property without losing your sanity requires a multi-faceted personality: a person who can wear many hats. She suggested we needed the skills and temperament of:

- a social worker
- a salesperson
- an investment counselor
- an advertising copywriter
- a psychiatrist
- a bouncer
- an interior decorator
- a paralegal

- an inventory clerk
- an executive secretary
- a bookkeeper
- a janitor
- a house painter
- a landscaper
- a general contractor
- ad nauseam

It was a long and intimidating list. As a rental property owner, you have an obvious choice: pay someone to manage the property or do it yourself. To adequately and profitably manage your rental yourself you need to do what professional property managers do.

To determine what professional property managers do for their fees, read any property management agreement. The manager will usually perform the following duties to one degree or another:

- rent, lease, operate, and manage the property
- use diligence in performing the contract
- prepare and submit statements of receipts, expenses, and charges
- accumulate reserves in a bank account
- deposit all rent receipts
- bond by fidelity bond employees who handle money
- advertise the rental
- display necessary "For Rent" signs
- sign, renew, or cancel leases
- collect rents, give receipts
- terminate tenancies
- evict tenants and recover possession of the rental when necessary
- recover rents and other sums due
- settle, compromise, or release rent disputes
- make or supervise repairs, alterations, or decorations
- purchase supplies and pay bills
- protect the property from damage
- prevent damage to life or personal property
- avoid penalties or fines
- maintain services to the tenants
- hire, supervise, and discharge all labor and employees

- appoint and retain attorneys, agents, or other necessary employees
- contract for electricity, gas, fuel, water, telephone, window cleaning, rubbish hauling, and any other necessary services
- pay loans, debts, taxes, special assessments, and insurance
- maintain complete and accurate records

That generally is what competent professional property managers should do for you as the owner of "income producing property." That list is also what you need to do for yourself, more or less, if you choose to manage your own rentals.

The property management agreement usually goes on to say that the owner is responsible for:

- any and all costs
- expenses
- attorney's fees
- suits
- liabilities
- damages or claim for damages relating to the management of the property

The owner's responsibilities also include carrying adequate insurance:

- public liability
- property damage
- workers' compensation

The owner is also responsible for paying the agent management and leasing fees. These fees can be either a flat fee or a percentage of gross or collected rents, depending on the type of property. In addition the owner must pay for "other than normal management functions." These might include:

- modernization
- refinancing
- fire restoration
- major rehabilitations
- obtaining income tax advice
- presenting petitions to planning or zoning committees
- advising on new construction
- other counseling

The 1986 Tax Reform Act

The 1986 Tax Reform Act has changed the way Americans look at ownership and management of real estate investments. As part of my research for this book, I wrote to the National Apartment Association, requesting information on the impact the 1986 Tax Reform Act would have on the rental business. In his reply, Charles H. Fritts, who was at that time tax and general counsel for the NAA sent a twenty-nine page study entitled "An Analysis of Real Estate Returns and Market Responses to the 1986 Tax Reform Act," by William B. Brueggeman (Corrigan Professor of Real Estate, Southern Methodist University) and Thomas G. Thibodeau (Assistant Professor of Real Estate and Regional Science, Southern Methodist University). The following information is a summary of portions of that report.

The report states that " while the Tax Reform Act of 1986 shifts much of the tax burden from individuals to corporations . . . it significantly reduces benefits to individuals making tax sheltered investments. Investors in income producing real estate have been especially targeted under the new legislation."

The most significant and far-reaching changes affect the limitation of losses, the repeal of the capital gain exclusion, and the reduction of depreciation expenses.

Tax rates

The new law provides for two basic tax brackets: a 15 percent rate for low- and moderate-income households and a 28 percent rate for middle- and upper-income households (rising to 33% in 1988 for some taxpayers).[1] The following is a summary of the major provisions of the tax law that affect real estate.

Active losses: The taxpayer that actively participates in the management of rental property can recognize up to $25,000 of losses. This $25,000 limit would be phased out as that taxpayer's income increases above $100,000. No losses from rental activities could be taken if the taxpayer's income exceeds $150,000.

Passive losses: The Act designates the business of renting property a per se passive activity regardless of the level of activity, extent of personal liability, or types of services performed. A loss from the operation of rental property cannot be used to offset income from

[1] The 15 percent rate applies to taxable income of up to $29,750.00. For incomes ranging from $29,750.00 to $71,900.00 the 28 percent is applied. *(Quoted verbatim from the Bruggeman-Thibodeau report.)*

wages and salary. There is a limited exception to this rule FOR AC-TIVE OWNERS with incomes of less than $150,000, allowing a five-year phase-in period.

Interest limitations: Investment interest expenses are deductible up to the amount of investment income received. This cap does not apply to mortgage interest on principal residences or vacation homes. Any passive loss is subtracted from investment income for purposes of determining the amount of income that is deductible.

Depreciation: The law lengthens the depreciation period for residential real estate to 27.5 years at a straight-line rate. Commercial property must be depreciated at a 31.5-year, straight-line rate. Certain transition rules also apply.

Capital gain exclusion: The 60% capital gains exclusion was repealed and the maximum individual tax rate on the sale of a capital asset is now 28%.

Alternative minimum tax: 21% rate including all passive losses. The difference of 40-year straight-line depreciation rate and 27.5-year rate is considered a preference item.

"At risk rules": Not applied to real estate if the lender is a third party.

Character of income or loss

The new law defines three categories of income or loss effectively reducing some traditional real estate tax benefits. The three categories are:

- Passive Income is income obtained from such passive invest-ment activities as a limited partnership interest in an asset held in trade or business, including income producing property.
- Portfolio Income is income from assets held for investment such as stocks, bonds, and commodities.
- Active Income includes personal service income.

The importance of the income categories is in determining how real estate income and losses will be classified and taxed.

The new tax law defines all rental activity as passive activity, however, actual classification of income and losses depends on the extent the investor participates in the management of the property.[2]

---

[2] A passive voice is defined as "Any activity: 1.) which involves the conduct of any trade or business (such as rentals); and 2.) in which the taxpayer does not materially participate (i.e.) interest in a limited partnership." (Page I 157 of Title V, Subtitle A,

Real estate income and losses will be categorized as passive income unless the taxpayer materially participates in the operation of the rental property.[3]

Talk to your tax advisor to determine the effects of all this on you and your real estate investments.

In deciding whether to manage your rentals yourself consider the following:

- Do you have the personality and temperament to manage your own rentals?
- Do you have the time?
- Do you have the necessary business skills?
- Do you possess enough knowledge of the business?
- What are the tax considerations?
- Do you really want to manage your own rentals?

Section 501a of the 1986 Tax Reform Act). "A taxpayer shall be treated as materially participating in an activity only if the taxpayer is involved in the operation on a regular basis which is regular, continuous, and substantial." To be a material participant, a taxpayer must have at least 10 percent interest in the real estate investment and must be involved in the operation of the property on a regular basis. Managing a rental property qualified as material participation, but simply ratifying decisions made by a property manager does not. A general partner in a syndication who has at least a 10 percent interest and also manages the property materially participates in the activity. *(Quoted verbatim from the Bruggeman-Thibodeau report.)*

[3] There is an exception to this rule for taxpayers who actively participate in passive activities. This would apply to a taxpayer who has at least a 10 percent interest and has some involvement in the properties' operation. The requirement for active participation is not as stringent as the requirement for material participation, however. Simply having a role in the decision-making process qualifies as active participation. For example, a taxpayer who has the responsibility of hiring the leasing agent for a property and who holds at least a 10 percent interest in the property is classified as an active participant. For active participants, the Act provides an exclusion of up to $25,000.00 provided the taxpayer's adjusted gross income is below $100,000.00. This exclusion is reduced ratably to zero as adjusted gross income increases to $150,000.00. *(Quoted verbatim from the Bruggeman-Thibodeau report.)*

CHAPTER 2

Keeping Good Records the Easy Way

One of the dullest, most easily neglected, and often most important areas of rental property ownership is record keeping. Without adequate and accessible records you increase your legal and financial risks considerably. The job of keeping your records need not be time-consuming drudgery. Simplify your record keeping as much as possible.

The following pointers will help you set up a simple, well organized, uniform information management system.

Why Keep Records?

The reasons for keeping records are important to remember, so you will not overburden yourself and your system with unnecessary information. Good record keeping is necessary to:

1. control and account for income and expenses
2. provide tax data (the IRS requires it)
3. accumulate data for operating efficiency
4. develop and enforce consistent policies
5. enable realistic budgeting
6. evaluate maintenance techniques
7. prepare for lawsuit defense

An Organized Workspace

The first step in getting your system organized is to establish a workspace. It need not be a complete office; sometimes a card table in the corner of your bedroom will be enough. The space should be away from the flow of traffic in your home. There are few things in life

more annoying than discovering the sticky remnants of a peanut but-
ter and jelly sandwich on one of your business files. Anacarria Myrrha,
a management information consultant, provides what she calls "a few
simple answers" to keep in mind when setting up a system that works
for you.

- Handle it once.
- Think retrieval.
- Get everything horizontal (not stacked).
- Establish a place for everything.
- Put everything in its place.
- When in doubt throw it out.
- Perfectionism is a waste of time.
- Schedule tasks for scheduled times.
- Organization is a process, not a goal.
- Work at that which you do best; hire someone to do the rest.

Information Management System Components

Ms. Myrrha recommends the following components for your information management system:

1. In/out tray: Use this for all incoming information so that it can
   be handled once on its way to the appropriate file or wastebasket.

2. On-desk action files: Label a set of folders and place them in
   a vertical file holder: To Do; To Pay; To Copy; To File; To
   Read; To Write. These folders are the second step in your
   paper flow.

3. Wastebasket: Throw away as much as you can. Keep only
   things you expect to refer to again that are not readily available to you elsewhere.

4. Junk drawer: Keep one place to accumulate all that extra
   stuff that we manage to collect.

5. Personal information management system: Select or create a
   looseleaf notebook system to help you record and retrieve
   information, and to manage your time and activities. I know
   some very active people who become total basket cases
   without their "brains" as they call these organizational tools.
   Your local stationery or office supply store probably has a se-
   lection of ready-made systems that range in price, content,

and quality; or you can make your own. Most systems include the following sections:

- monthly calendar
- week-at-a-glance
- "To Do" lists
- projects
- agendas
- finances
- goals
- journal
- names and addresses

6. Wall calendar: Hang your calendar where it's easily visible for quick reference. On it, note long-range plans, major deadlines and events.

7. Follow-up system: This "tickler" system reminds you of important dates automatically. It can be any one of several formats:

- calendar in your notebook
- action file folder
- set of monthly file folders
- card file dividers

Whatever format you use, keep a separate sheet or card for each month as well as day by day or week by week. File by the month. These files are not for document storage. They are reminders of lease expirations, warranties, insurance renewals, scheduled maintenance, rent increases and other important dates.

8. Filing system: Create a filing system that is simple, sensible, and standardized so that other people can find things, if necessary. There is more information on how to set up a system, what to put in it, and how to check it later in this chapter.

9. Travel folder: This is a four- or six-part divided, expandable folder. Since owners and managers often need specific information at the property, this system eliminates the need to remove your files from your filing cabinet. There's more on the specifics of this invaluable tool later.

10. Storage area: Transfer all out-of-date records from your central files to storage boxes. Carefully label these boxes with contents and dates.

Filing System

A-Z index

Whatever way you categorize your filed information, it is important to know where to look for it so that you and others can locate files quickly and easily. The first file folder in the file drawer should contain a file index. Keeping such a list is easy if you have a computer; more time consuming if you don't, of course.

Forms and legal notices

The number of properties and units you own or manage will determine the quantity of blank forms and notices you need to keep on hand and how you file them. I keep each of the following in a separate file. You may get by with a few of each in one folder.

- Applications
- Rental Agreements
- Leases
- Addenda
- House Rules
- Move In/Out Checklist
- Move In/Out Condition Reports
- Cleaning Checklist
- Landlord/Tenant pamphlets or brochures
- Maintenance Service Requests
- Three Day Notice To Pay Rent
- Three Day Notice To Correct Breach
- Three Day Notice for Breach of Contract
- Thirty Day Notice
- Notice of Abandonment
- Notice to Reclaim Abandoned Property
- Notice of Change of Terms of Tenancy

Samples of each of these forms are in the appendix, along with a brief statement about their purpose, how to prepare them, copies needed, service requirements (if applicable), and some precautions about the use of each. These are only samples; be sure that the forms you use apply in your jurisdiction. Your best sources of up-to-date forms are your local apartment association or board of realtors.

Categorizing your files

However you categorize your files, be consistent. I find it useful to subdivide files for each property into four general areas:

1. Administrative, to include:
   - correspondence
   - insurance
   - escrow documents
   - advertising
   - dead files (alphabetically)
     — all former residents
     — all rejected or withdrawn applications

2. Financial, to include:
   - bank records
   - tenant ledgers
   - budgets
   - income and expense records
   - financing information
   - tax forms and information

3. Property files, to include:
   - floor plan
   - property information (see Chapter 8),
   - electrical and plumbing schematics
   - emergency information, such as
     — turn-off valve locations
     — alarm system
     — smoke detector information
     — emergency procedures
     — emergency phone numbers
   - equipment
   - suppliers and contractors
   - warranties
   - maintenance schedules

4. Resident File, by unit, to include:
   - Application
   - Rental Agreement
   - Move In/Out Condition Report
   - all correspondence
   - all communications

This outline is not inclusive. You will need to create categories and files to suit your property and your situation. Be clear on what you need to file and where to file it.

Again, I am grateful to Anacarria Myrrha of Simple Systems for providing the Filing System Checklist and the Filing System Reorganization Instructions, which follow.

Filing System Checklist

1. Are items found quickly when needed?
2. Are files correctly and adequately labeled?
3. Are files categorized in a consistent manner?
4. Is there a procedure for setting up new files and labeling them?
5. Is one person responsible for setting up new files?
6. Is any useless material being filed?
7. Is there a plan to avoid duplication?
8. Is the number of papers in each folder limited to 50 or less?
9. Are staples used instead of paper clips?
10. Are paper fasteners used in folders?
11. Are the left and right sides of the folder used to advantage?
12. Is there a method for cross referencing information?
13. Are fiscal and/or calendar year records separated and stored separately?
14. Is there a record retention system?
15. Are category divider guides used in file drawers?
16. Is color coding used?
17. Is there a master index of files?
18. Is there a procedure for returning materials to the filing system?

Filing System Reorganization

Supplies

Purchase or have on-hand the following basic filing system supplies:

- vertical file-folder holder
- letter-size file folders with third-cut or straight-cut tabs
- yellow "Post-It" notes, size 3 x 3
- colored file-folder labels

- letter-size pressboard file drawer dividers
- self-adhesive fasteners
- two-hole punch
- boxes for storage

Procedure

1. Set up action files. Use colored folders for easy visual reference.

2. File all existing folders into current filing system. If there is a question about what or where, write notes on the outside of folder for future reference.

3. Sort through loose papers. Throw away all unnecessary items.

4. File all papers that can be put into existing folders.

5. Make a list of major categories to be used in new system. See above for samples.

6. Remove all hanging files from file drawers.

7. Label pressboard dividers with major categories and place in drawer in alphabetical order. Use temporary labels.

8. Arrange existing file folders in drawers behind appropriate file dividers. Alphabetize the folders within each category.

9. Sort remaining papers. Place in used file folders and label with temporary labels. File alphabetically into system. (Note: Categories and names of folders may change as you create a system unique to your needs).

10. Review files and make any needed changes or corrections.

11. Decide on color-coding system.

12. Type labels, place on new file folders, and transfer documents.

Travel Folder

The travel folder is portable, unlike your office filing system. In it are copies of all documents you may need at the property for tenants, appraisers, contractors, real estate people, landscapers and so forth. Consistent with my filing system, I divide my travel folder into the following sections: administrative, financial, property, resident.

For larger properties I add sections for a directory and advertising. In the directory are resident lists, vendor lists, phone numbers, fire plans, emergency information, and anything else I might need to have quickly. This system works well for any size property, from single-family residences to multi-unit projects. I keep my travel folders at my desk for quick reference when they are not needed in the field. Periodically, you'll have to go through your travel folder and discard outdated information.

Operating your rental business is a lot easier with a well organized information management system. Remember to:

Keep It Simple.

Cover Your Assets.

CHAPTER 3

Budgeting By the Numbers

Budgets have a poor reputation as financial tools because they are often ill-conceived and ineffectively used.

A budget is only as good as the assumptions upon which it is based. A workable budget is more than a challenging academic exercise. It is a practical operating tool that enables you to establish a spending plan that lets you know how you are doing. As a rental owner, you need to budget with care and common sense. Remembering the reasons for budgeting will help you prepare a financial guideline that works for you and your property.

A budget:

1. establishes a spending plan

2. helps plan capital expenditures

3. helps control expenses

4. provides ongoing comparisons

Types of Budgets

There are a variety of budgeting methods.

Annual net operating income (NOI) projection is an estimate of annual income less itemized operating expenses. At the end of the year you can see how well you did. It is not a very practical working tool as there is no way to make periodic adjustments.

Monthly net operating income projection allows you to make monthly adjustments. You can also include year to date figures and comparisons to previous years expenses.

Annual cash flow budget shows you yearly cash flow by subtracting mortgage payments from net operating income. Again, annual calculations do not allow for periodic adjustments.

Monthly cash flow budget lets you know how much money you'll have each month. This allows you to plan more accurately for seasonal considerations such as fuel or snow removal, and large ticket items like real estate taxes and capital improvements.

Comparative budgets allow you to compare actual monthly and year-to-date income and expenses with your projections. This type of format takes a monthly cash flow budget a step further. For smaller properties quarterly comparisons are sufficient.

Budgeting is especially useful in controlling variable expenses, such as advertising, repairs, maintenance, and supplies. Noncontrollable (or fixed) expenses include debt service, utilities, taxes, and insurance.

Budget Guidelines

Minimum categories

The fewer categories there are in your budget, the less variations will show up. On the other hand, the more categories you have, the easier it will be to spot fluctuations. For example, you could choose to show separate accounts for heating fuel, gas, electricity, water, and sewer. If you miscalculate one or more categories, your budget will show variations. If, however, you combine all these expenses under the heading of utilities, the fluctuations will tend to level out. The following is a list of the minimum categories you'll need. You can add sub-headings to these as you see fit.

- utilities
- services (such as trash collection and pest control)
- supplies
- payroll
- advertising
- administration (management)
- legal
- accounting
- insurance
- real estate taxes
- repairs and maintenance
- miscellaneous

Use rounded numbers

Rounding out the figures you use allows for reasonable variations. For instance if you set a budget amount at $50.00, you could reasonably expect the actual expenditure to be several dollars more or less than that. If large discrepancies occur regularly, change the amount projected. Budgets are, after all, only estimates.

Use current figures

If you allow for inflation or known cost increase say so in your assumptions.

Project on the high side

Expenses seem to have a way of always being a little more than we anticipate. Budgeting on the low side may make your projections look great on paper, but at the end of the year you might find yourself a little short. Be as realistic as you can.

Prepare your budgets early

For monthly budgets, have your projections prepared midway through the previous month. Yearly budgets should be ready a month in advance.

Preparing A Budget Step-by-Step

Step 1: scheduled gross income

The first step is to estimate the annual gross income your property will generate at 100 percent occupancy. (To determine a realistic "market rent" see the section entitled "Know Your Market" in Chapter Eight.) If you have a resident manager include the value of his or her unit in your calculations. Add any other income your property brings in, such as parking fees, and laundry or vending machines. Do not include security deposits (it's not your money). The total possible income is your Scheduled Gross Income.

Step 2: effective gross income

The second step is to determine an allowance for vacancy and rent loss. Subtract this figure from the scheduled gross income to arrive at Effective Gross Income.

Step 3: net operating income

The third step is to add up your projected annual expenses (excluding debt service). Subtract your estimated expenses from the effective gross income to arrive at Net Operating Income (NOI).

Step 4: cash flow

The fourth step, if you are preparing an annual cash flow budget, is to subtract your annual debt service (principal and interest) from the annual net operating income to determine Annual Cash Flow.

Step 5: breakdowns and adjustments

The fifth step, if you are preparing a monthly or quarterly cash flow budget, is to break down your annual figures to quarterly or monthly figures, making the necessary seasonal adjustments.

Step 6: comparisons

A sixth step, if you'd like to compare your budgeted expenses with your actual expenses, is to create and keep up-to-date a form similar to this one:

COMPARATIVE BUDGET AND WORKSHEET

Property: _____

Year: _____

Budget Mo/Yr to Dt/Yr	Chart of Accounts INCOME	Actual Expenses Mo/Yr to Dt/ Yr
___ ___ ___	Scheduled Rent	___ ___ ___
___ ___ ___	Less	___ ___ ___
___ ___ ___	Vacancy	___ ___ ___
___ ___ ___	Rent Loss	___ ___ ___
___ ___ ___	Effective Rent	___ ___ ___
	EXPENSES	
___ ___ ___	Administration	___ ___ ___
___ ___ ___	Accounting	___ ___ ___
___ ___ ___	Legal	___ ___ ___
___ ___ ___	Insurance	___ ___ ___
___ ___ ___	Advertising	___ ___ ___
___ ___ ___	Real Estate Taxes	___ ___ ___
___ ___ ___	Payroll	___ ___ ___
___ ___ ___	Utilities	___ ___ ___

___	___	___	Supplies	___	___	___
___	___	___	Repairs & Maintenance	___	___	___
___	___	___	Contract Services	___	___	___
___	___	___	Miscellaneous	___	___	___
___	___	___	TOTAL EXPENSES	___	___	___
___	___	___	NET OPERATING INCOME	___	___	___
___	___	___	DEBT SERVICE	___	___	___
___	___	___	CASH FLOW	___	___	___

Prepared By _____   Date _____

Remember, you can add as many categories, or "line items," as you feel you need. Large apartment complexes and homeowners associations use hundreds of line items in their budgets, including reserves for major improvements and replacements. If you choose to budget reserves, add a line just after net operating income.

Other Financial Records

Your budget serves as a financial game plan. There are a few other records which will help you control your income and expenses and provide needed tax information.

Your bookkeeper or tax accountant will help you establish a set of records to:

- record the original property acquisition
- provide an accounting record for tax purposes
- establish a depreciation schedule
- determine a basis for your particular financial position

The following records can handle up to 100 units or more. Keep a separate set for each property. If you are just starting to build your real estate empire, you may not need all of them initially. Consult your accountant and use your own judgment to determine what works best for you.

Rent receipt

Receipt books in triplicate can be purchased from any office supply store. Give or send the original copy to your tenant when you receive the rent. Attach the duplicate to the tenant ledger, then check the total receipts with your bank deposit and keep with duplicate bank deposit. Keep the triplicate in the book as a permanent record.

Bank deposit

Use bank deposit forms that provide space to list each check or money order separately. Prepare in duplicate (triplicate if you have a manager). The original goes to the bank with your deposit. Keep the duplicate with the corresponding rent receipts.

Tenant ledger

Prepare a new ledger card for each new tenant. Post all rents from rent receipts and expenditures from work orders. When the tenant has moved out of the unit, file the ledger in your inactive file.

Monthly rent report

A columnar monthly income record is compiled from your rent receipts. It can be prepared by you (in duplicate) or your manager (in triplicate). The original is for your files; duplicate goes to your accountant; triplicate is retained by the manager (if applicable). Column headings can include unit number, prior balance due, tenant name, gross rent, deposit amount, deposit date, receipt number, rent collected, deposit collected, other collected comments.

Disbursement record

On a columnar work sheet, you or your bookkeeper post each disbursement monthly from your checkbook. Column headings are the same as the line items listed under expenses in your budget chart of accounts. All columns must be totaled and cross balanced.

Operating statement

The operating statement is prepared by you or your bookkeeper from the monthly rent report and the disbursement record. The comparative budget worksheet shown previously doubles as a monthly, year-to-date, and annual operating statement. Your careful monthly review of this report will help you locate areas that may need attention. It is an excellent operations guide.

Work order

The work order is used to control all repairs other than routine maintenance and cleaning. It can also be used to document necessary cleaning and repair expenses to be deducted from a security deposit after a tenant moves out. Prepare in duplicate or triplicate. Your repair or cleaning person then documents work completed, labor and material costs. You retain the original when issued. The completed duplicate is attached to the tenant ledger and the completed triplicate is kept by your manager. This form is excellent documentation of repair costs.

Petty cash report

If you use a petty cash fund, you'll need an envelope that documents expenditures and balances. Keep vouchers, invoices, and cash in the envelope.

Inventory control forms

Use lined 3 x 5 cards to control inventories of appliances, furniture, maintenance supplies, paint, tools, and equipment. As each item is stored or taken out, note on your card: number of pieces, date, where it came from, where it went, and new balances.

Liability control

Liability control data can be kept on a standard 3 x 5 or 5 x 8 ruled card, prepared by you or your bookkeeper at the beginning of each month. Use this form for each property to record: the lender, the loan amount, interest rate, term monthly payment, and payment due date. It also records your payments, showing: date, check number, amount paid, principle, interest, tax and insurance impounds, and balances.

Cheer up! Your lender may supply all of this information to you in a monthly statement.

Prepackaged bookkeeping systems

If you find all of these forms mind boggling, there's still hope. Office supply stores carry a variety of bookkeeping systems and formats specifically designed for rental properties. The introduction to the Ideal Rental Property Record says that it can be used for apartments, rental houses, duplexes, office buildings, and store buildings. It says that it is "a complete, simplified, up-to-date bookkeeping system and tax record all in one book." Pegboard systems allow one entry to be recorded on several forms. Confer with your bookkeeper to see if one of these systems will work for you.

Computers and programs

These days more and more families and small businesses are using computers. If you have access to a personal computer, your recordkeeping and bookkeeping can be infinitely easier. With some combination of word processing, spreadsheet, and/or data base programs, your possibilities are practically endless. In researching this book, I came across a variety of programs designed specifically for property management. Most, unfortunately, are too complicated and too expensive to be used effectively for a small rental business. You don't need a "smart bomb" when a fly swatter will do. In light of this, the publisher and I are looking into the possibility of developing *For Rent By Owner* rental software that can provide complete recordkeeping and accounting for small rental businesses. Such a program should be easy to learn and use, and be versatile, flexible, and cost effective. Stay tuned.

If you are interested in appropriate software for your rental business, your local apartment or rental housing association may be able to help you.

CHAPTER 4

Insurance:
Covering Your Assets

Unless you live in a vacuum, you are well aware that insurance costs have risen drastically over the past few years. This rise is generally attributed to a claims-conscious public. Even if you have "deep pockets" you'll need good comprehensive insurance to cover your assets.

The first step in getting appropriate insurance coverage is to get a reliable, knowledgeable insurance agent or broker. Choose a broker or agent who represents many different companies unless you have personal reasons for sticking to a one-company person. After analyzing your particular situation, the insurance agent can shop around and advise you on the best policy or policies. A thorough inspection of your property will enable your agent to advise you on ways to reduce certain hazards and risks; and your insurance costs.

Types of coverage

There are three general areas of potential loss that your insurance needs to cover: property damage, liability, and rent loss.

The types of insurance generally available vary considerably in coverage and cost.

- Fire Insurance is the most basic and is required by all lenders to protect their interests.
- Extended Coverage is also a basic policy and usually covers loss due to: lightning, wind, hail, explosion, riot, smoke, vehicles, and aircraft.
- Vandalism and malicious mischief coverage is also considered essential.
- Comprehensive general liability policies protect you against personal injury or property damage to others while on your property (tenants, guests, visitors, and the general public).
- Multi-peril or package policies can include all of the above and

are less expensive than individual policies.

- Workers compensation insurance is required in most states if you have employees. Your resident manager is usually considered an employee, even though you might have an independent contractor agreement with him or her. Even the neighborhood kid who mows your lawn may be considered an employee under certain circumstances.

Other specialized types of coverage you might consider include:

- contents insurance for your personal property on the premises such as refrigerator, stove, or any furniture (does not include your tenants' personal property)
- boiler and machinery coverage
- plate glass insurance
- sprinkler leakage coverage
- fidelity bond or a blanket crime policy
- auto insurance
- catastrophe endorsements for flood, earthquake, or other localized natural disasters

Ask your agent if your rentals can be covered under your homeowner's coverage or if you need some sort of landlord/tenant policy. Also check into an "inflation guard" endorsement.

Deductibles

Most losses are not total losses. If you are willing to pay for your smaller amounts of damage, the exposure to your insurance company will be less, and so will your insurance payment or premium. Deductible amounts can range from $100 to thousands of dollars. If you have a deductible amount of $500, then the insurance company will deduct or subtract $500 from your claim settlement. If your damage amounts to less than your deductible amount, you should not report the claim. Deductible clauses are similar to co-insurance clauses in that you are essentially "self-insuring" up to the amount of your deductible, making you a co-insurer with your insurance company. One difference is that deductibles are fixed amounts, while "co-insurance" is a percentage of value.

Co-insurance

Co-insurance clauses of insurance policies are easily misunderstood. These provisions were designed to encourage policy holders to carry adequate amounts of fire and extended coverage insurance on their properties. Here's how they work:

Insurance companies figure that approximately 20 percent of any structure will not be destroyed even in a "total loss." That 20 percent includes such things as foundations, heavy boilers, water and sewer lines, and so forth. Based on this assumption, insurance companies require owners to carry a policy covering 80 percent of the value. With an 80 percent co-insurance clause the insurer will cover damages up to the specified amount. For example: If your property had a value of $100,000, you would be required to carry $80,000 worth of insurance with an 80 percent co-insurance provision. If you do carry the required $80,000, then the insurance company will pay you in full for any covered damage up to the policy limit. On a $10,000 loss, they would pay $10,000. If you carried only $60,000 of insurance, they would pay you only 60/80 of the loss or ¾ or 75 percent. On a loss of $10,000, they would pay you $7500. Here's the formula:

$$\frac{\text{Insurance carried}}{\text{Insurance required}} = \frac{\text{Percentage of loss}}{\text{Paid by insurer}}$$

Using the figures from the above example, it would look like this:

$$\frac{\$80,000}{\$80,000} = \frac{1}{1 \text{ or } 100\% \text{ of } \$10,000 = \$10,000}$$

and

$$\frac{\$60,000}{\$80,000} = \frac{3}{4 \text{ or } 75\% \text{ of } \$10,000 = \$7,500}$$

It is important to keep your insurance up to the required percentage of the value of your property. If your property is worth $100,000 and under an 80 percent co-insurance provision you carry $80,000 worth of insurance, you are 100 percent covered up to an $80,000 loss.

As the years go by, your property increases in value. It is now worth $150,000, but you are still only carrying $80,000. That same $10,000 loss will now look like this:

$$\frac{\$80,000}{\$120,000 \ (80\% \text{ of } \$150,000)} = \frac{2}{3} \text{ or } 66\% \text{ of } \$10,000 = \$6,666$$

Checking and adjusting your insurance coverage periodically is essential to avoid being underinsured.

Who is insured?

You, as the owner of the property, are the "named insured." Your on-site manager, any employees, and any managing agent, need to be covered as "additional insured" for certain types of coverage. Your lenders will also be "additional insured" on any type of coverage that may affect their collateral, the property, in the amount of their liability, which is the mortgage balance.

Damage or loss claims: what to do

One of the most important steps you can take is to insist on being supplied a claims reporting package at the time you place the insurance. Then, when you need to file a claim:

1. Phone your insurance company or agent immediately.

2. Send a written report as soon as possible.

3. Protect the property.

4. Take necessary steps to avoid additional liability or damage.

5. Separate the undamaged property from the damaged property.

6. Document the damage or loss in detail, showing costs and values.

Renters insurance

Very few tenants carry insurance to cover their belongings in the event of a loss, or to protect themselves of liability should they be responsible for damage. If they have thought of insurance at all, they often assume that the property owner's insurance will cover them and/or their losses. Be sure to tell them it is not so. Point out to them their risks and advise them to get a renters' policy.

CHAPTER 5

Everybody's Rights and Responsibilities

There are as many definitions of landlord/tenant rights and responsibilities as there are states to define them. Some general categories are included in the landlord/tenant laws of most states, but to compare them would take volumes. The following sources will help you locate information about rights and responsibilities in your locality that you as a rental owner need to be aware of.

- State legislators
- Housing offices
- Libraries
- Apartment associations
- Tenant organizations
- Consumer awareness groups
- Your lawyer

Tenant rights; owner responsibilities

Tenant rights and owner responsibilities are flip sides of the same coin. If one party has a right, then the other party has a responsibility to honor that right. Depending on your point of view tenant right laws are usually described as liberal or conservative, strict, lenient, tenant-oriented, and so forth. Regardless of how they are written, or for whom, most states have legislation covering the following general areas.

- habitability standards
- peaceful and quiet enjoyment of the premises
- legal eviction
- security deposit refund

"Habitable condition" and "good repair" are terms that are

found in many landlord/tenant statutes, but what do they mean? An owner who never sees the property might define "habitable" in a very different way than does the person who lives there. Since opinions do differ so widely on this subject, the states that have habitability standards have enlightened us with some guidelines. They usually regulate the following:

- weather protection (roof, walls, windows, doors)
- plumbing
- running water (hot, cold)
- lighting
- heating
- garbage and sewage
- and whatever else "they" feel is appropriate for the health and well-being of the tenant.

Many states also have statutes regulating security and other health and safety considerations. Many states and local jurisdictions require smoke detectors and sprinkler systems to be installed in every residence. Be aware that habitability standards are subject to change (and to definition) and keep yourself informed. "Lack of habitability" is often a valid defense in eviction proceedings.

"Quiet enjoyment of the premises by the tenant" grants to him certain degrees of privacy. Here again, there is a full spectrum of interpretations of what that might mean. Learn the statutes in your jurisdiction, and what they mean.

Violation of these rights are usually defined as harassment.

You can, of course, evict your tenant for non-payment of rent (usually). Make sure you follow the legal procedure for your jurisdiction. The procedure may be simple and quick, or complicated and time consuming. Whatever it is, don't take shortcuts. Legal eviction is one of your tenants' rights. Don't make up your own rules based on what you believe is fair or right. Follow the rules (regardless of your opinion of them) and you will save yourself a lot of grief.

Security deposit regulations cover everything from the amount you can charge to what can be deducted and when the deposit needs to be returned. Payment of interest on security deposits held by an owner is the subject of much discussion in many state and local governments. Keep yourself informed and play by the rules. Respect your tenants' rights, whatever they are, whether you like it or not.

Landlord rights; tenant responsibilities

The rights of owners are the responsibilities of the tenant, just as the tenants' rights are the owners' responsibility. There are four basic rights an owner has.

1. Timely receipt of rent
2. Tenant agrees not to damage premises
3. Compliance with written agreements
4. Surrender of premises at end of term

Common sense, yes, but also usually the law. Other rights and responsibilities can be agreed to in a legal contract, such as a lease or rental agreement. A party to a contract cannot sign away his legal rights. Good, up-to-date rental documents will help protect both your rights and those of your tenants.

No-nos

During evictions, there are some activities that are considered "self-help." Some states allow them; most don't.

Legal or not, they are not recommended, as they may only aggravate an already tense situation. These self-help remedies include locking your tenant out, shutting off utilities, and other devious deeds. Use of these tactics can be self-defeating. Angry, frustrated tenants have been known to inflict major damage on property and person.

Baggage lien laws

Many states' civil codes contain what are commonly referred to as "Baggage Lien Laws." These laws allow an owner of rentals to impound a tenants' personal property in lieu of past due rent. Actual enforcement of these laws can be complicated, time consuming, and expensive (in more ways than one). Often, notice requirements allow the tenant to stash the goods by the time the owner or his agent can get to them. No goods, no confiscation; process defeated. Even if your state or locality does have a baggage lien law on the books, it may not be practical to use.

A few years ago I had the opportunity to tour some apartment complexes with a client in the Dallas, Texas area.

It was shortly after the Dallas Cowboys were in the Super Bowl. The management of one of the projects had chosen to enforce the baggage lien law on their delinquent renters by confiscating their television sets during Super Bowl week. The result was pandemo-

nium. The storeroom, where the sets and other confiscated goods
were kept, was broken into, sets stolen or destroyed, the office was
vandalized, records were burned and shredded, and many of the tenants threatened a rent strike. There is a moral to this story: Don't
mess with the TV sets of Dallas Cowboy fans when their team is in
the Super Bowl, even if the law says you can. If you do have a workable baggage lien law where your rentals are, use it judiciously.

Right of entry

You may not necessarily enter your rental anytime you choose.
State laws restrict your right to enter to certain circumstances and
with "reasonable notice," and often only at specified times. Usually,
you may enter the rental for the following reasons:

- emergency
- necessary repairs
- tenant abandons or surrenders premises
- court order

In addition to your right to enter the rental as established by the law,
be sure to include in your lease or rental agreement a clause allowing you
the right to enter with reasonable notice, at reasonable times for:

- maintenance inspections
- showing the rental to prospective tenants
- showing the rental to prospective purchasers or lenders

You may be required to provide written notice prior to entry.
What does "reasonable notice" mean in your state? If twenty-four
hours is considered reasonable notice, when does the time begin to
run? Does it begin when you mail or post the notice, or does it begin
when the tenant has knowledge of the notice? Does the tenant have
to cooperate?

What can you do if the tenant changes the locks, and refuses to
give you a new key? Can you hire a locksmith? If so, who pays? Can
you force your way into the rental? If you do, you may be subject to
criminal penalties.

In addition to those problems, you may face an invasion of privacy claim by entering a tenant's unit. Also, you may face the claim
that valuable personal property is missing following an entry by you
or your agent. Even when you have permission and authority to enter
the rental, always have a witness present.

Be very cautious when entering a rental. Legal entanglements involving right to enter range from harassment and invasion of privacy to grand theft and even justifiable homicide. The following are recommended procedures for entering a rental unit:

1. Give written notice whenever possible.
2. Verify appointed time with tenant by phone or in person.
3. Ring doorbell or knock loudly.
4. Open door slightly and call tenant's name.
5. Enter cautiously with a witness.
6. Knock on any closed interior doors before opening.
7. Post a note at the door advising that you are inside.
8. Take every action you can think of to let your tenant know when you will be there and what you will be doing.

Repair and deduct statutes

Repair and deduct statutes allow a tenant, after notifying the owner of a defect, to make the repair and deduct the cost from the rent. These laws are in effect in many jurisdictions and many others are considering them. The laws typically place restrictions on the tenant's right to deduct repair costs from his rent. There are also certain procedures which must be followed. Generally, the law can be used only for certain defects that affect the habitability of the rental. The tenant cannot deduct repair costs if he has interfered with your attempts to make the repair, or if he negligently caused the damage. The tenant must give you written notice of the repair he wishes, then wait a "reasonable" period of time for you to respond. Reasonable depends on the circumstances. The reasonable time he would have to wait for running water, for instance, would be different from the reasonable time he could expect to wait for an air conditioner repair in January. The law also limits the number of times a tenant may repair and deduct.

Some jurisdictions, depending on the circumstances, allow the tenant to legally withhold the rent or a portion of it until repairs are made.

Tenants can also either report deficiencies to the authorities, sue you, and/or move out, depending on the situation. Good rental management dictates that you communicate with your tenants and handle problems as they arise rather than allow them to handle you.

The best way to avoid tenants' rights disputes is to make sure both you and your tenants are aware of everyone's rights and responsibilities. Disagreements may still arise, but you can minimize them.

CHAPTER 6

All About Rents and Deposits

My trusty desktop dictionary defines rent as "a fixed amount payable at a stated time by a tenant to a landlord for the use of property." Look at the components of that definition and you get a clear picture of the rental business.

- a fixed amount
- payable
- at a specified time
- by a tenant
- to a landlord
- for the use of property

Types of rent

Typically, rents are due and payable in advance on the first day of each month. Don't make the mistake of charging your rent every 30 days from the move-in date. This can be confusing for everyone and complicates your record-keeping. Rents are calculated on a monthly basis, not on a 30 day basis.

If your tenants should question you as to why they need to pay in advance, rather than after the rental period, there is an answer. Rent is a purchase of time for the use of your space. Time is not recoverable. If a tenant does not pay his rent on time, the owner is deprived of the chance to rent that space for that past period of time. Collecting past due rent is a slow, expensive, and iffy process. You have no guarantee of collecting. Collecting rent in advance is one tradition that favors the landlord.

Many residential and commercial leases provide for an *aggregate rent*, or total term rental amount, which is payable in monthly installments. This obligates the tenant for the entire amount due for the full lease period. These leases usually specify that the full sum is due and payable if an installment is missed. The courts do not necessarily uphold these acceleration clauses.

A *graduated rent* provision may be used in longer term leases to establish periodic rent increases. Be sure to specify the date and amount of each increase to avoid conflict and confusion. This technique is useful in a soft (not much demand) rent market. Lower the initial rental amount so that it is very attractive to prospective tenants, then you can provide for periodic upward adjustments. Explain to your prospects what you are doing and why. Since people are usually most concerned with immediate costs, they understand the necessity of a graduated rent and do not normally object.

Another form of graduated rent is often used in student housing. Two rent levels are established: one for the ten-month school term and a discounted rate for the summer. The summer discount provides incentive for the student to either stay or sub-lease his unit and allows the owner to eliminate an expensive vacancy period.

Another rent variation that is used in college towns is a *head rent*. Rent is charged per person, rather than per unit. Use of this system can cause discrimination, collection, and bookkeeping problems that you may want to avoid. An alternative in a student-oriented market is to rent to one person or family who is responsible for the full rent and allow selective sub-leasing.

How much rent?

Normally you can charge whatever you can get for rent. The only limiting factors are supply, demand, and rent control ordinances. Determining supply and demand and how they affect market rents is fully discussed in Chapter Eight.

One major factor that tends to limit the supply of rental housing in the future is the Tax Reform Act of 1986. The Act took away much of the incentive for new residential multi-family construction. The Tax Reform Act generally caused rents to increase and created additional pressure to impose rent controls. The threat of the imposition of rent control is very real in many localities where there is more demand than supply.

Rent control

Rent control laws limit the amount of rent an owner can charge. They vary considerably in the cities and counties that have them. Differences typically are in how they are administered, registration requirements, exemptions, and the formulas used to determine rent levels and allowable increases.

Most ordinances do not cover all rental housing within their jurisdiction. Often they exempt owner occupied buildings with two, three, or four rental units, single family residences, some new construction, transient housing, and so forth.

Rent control ordinances are usually administered by a rent control board which is appointed by the city council or county board of supervisors. Some are elected.

Many rent control districts require owners to register with the rent control agency. This allows the agency more control of the units under its jurisdiction. Some jurisdictions allow tenants to withhold rent if the unit is not registered. Other agencies have no registration requirements.

Formulas used to determine rents and periodic adjustments also vary quite a bit. There are two basic methods of determining rent increases. One is periodic general increases as determined by the rent control board. The second involves a petition to the board for a rent increase based on increased costs. Tenants also have the right to petition for a decrease in rent level.

Some rent control jurisdictions have what is called "vacancy decontrol." This provision allows rent control only until the tenant moves out. After that the owner is allowed to charge a market rent. Since most people move from a rental every two years or so, vacancy decontrol allows rents to rise to their market level just a little slower than they would without rent control. Rent control proponents claim that vacancy decontrol is a poor feature because it tends to encourage owners to either evict tenants or make life miserable for them so that they'll move voluntarily. However, jurisdictions that have vacancy decontrols also tend to have eviction protection ordinances. These provisions require that a tenant be evicted only for "just cause," such as nonpayment of rent, or otherwise breaking the rental agreement. Some jurisdictions prohibit "retaliatory eviction." Evictions are more thoroughly covered in Chapter Ten.

A final word on rent control: If you have rent control ordinances in your city, or if they are being considered, join and support organizations that lobby against them, such as the local chapter of the National Apartment Association. Please do not resort to the sleazy tactics that give landlords an often well-deserved poor reputation.

Rental Agreements

The renting of residential property forms a contract between the owner and the tenant. There are three types of rental contracts:

1. Oral (or verbal) Rental Agreement
2. Written Rental Agreement
3. Written Lease

Verbal rental agreements

A verbal rental agreement is made without writing down the terms of the agreement. The owner or manager simply agrees verbally with the tenant on the basic terms of the rental. In its simplest form a verbal rental agreement includes the following:

1. Owner agrees to rent to the renter.
2. Renter agrees to pay a specified amount for rent.
3. Occupancy date is agreed upon.
4. Length of rental time is agreed upon.
5. Renter pays owner rent.
6. Owner gives renter the key.
7. Renter moves in.

Life should be so simple! The occupancy by the renter with the owner's permission is considered legal notice that there is a rental agreement in force.

The length of time between rent payments usually determines the time needed for termination of the agreement by either party. For example, if the rent is paid monthly, 30 days notice is required to terminate the tenancy. The same time period is required for notice of any changes in the tenancy such as rent increases.

Problems arise when the terms are verbal and there is a dispute. Often, a judge must decide who to believe in a disagreement. It is always better to have rental agreements in writing so as to clarify and document terms and conditions of the rental. Also, all parties to the agreement should sign it. Even if the renters are married, or "domestic partners," both should sign.

Written rental agreements

The written agreement (a lease or rental agreement) is evidence and proof of a binding legal relationship between the owner and the tenant of a property. It is a legal contract. Contract law varies from state to state. The sample lease and rental agreement in the appendix of this book were adapted from a variety of sources. As of the printing of this book, they represent valid and up-to-date contracts in the state of California only. They are included in this book strictly as examples of forms available for use in the rental business. Be sure that the forms you use in your rental business are up-to-date in the state where your rentals are. Any form you use should be approved by your attorney.

A written rental agreement usually specifies a month-to-month tenancy where either party can terminate the agreement with 30-days notice. Other provisions typically include:

- description of the premises
- the amount of rent and when payable
- an occupancy date
- duration of the agreement
- designation of the parties involved
- the number of occupants
- who pays which utilities
- signatures of all occupants
- rent increases with notice equal to the rent period

Leases

A written lease agreement is similar in terms and conditions to the rental agreement except that the period of tenancy is specified. During the specified period, the property owner may not increase the rent or evict the tenant unless the tenant breaks a condition of the lease. Leases are generally considered favorable to the tenant.

There are six essential elements needed to create a valid lease. They are:

1. the correct names and signatures of legally competent parties
2. an identifiable description of the premises and its condition
3. consideration
4. legality of use
5. beginning and ending dates
6. rights and obligations of the parties

What do each of those requirements mean?

Legally competent contracting parties. The competency of a person to enter into contracts is determined by state law and may vary. Consider these examples:

Minors are considered incompetent to enter into contractual relationships in all jurisdictions. However, definitions of a minor may vary. Usually it is anyone under the age of 18. Contracts signed by minors are voidable, but not necessarily void or invalid. That means that the adult is obligated to the terms and conditions of the contract, but the minor may void the agreement anytime he chooses without penalty; a lopsided arrangement that should be avoided.

Insane or senile persons generally have the same protections as minors. If a question of insanity or senility is a possible consideration, have a doctor or other competent party witness the agreement and sign a statement regarding the competency of the person. Better yet, avoid the whole thing, if you can.

Corporations are regarded as persons (individual entities) competent to enter into contracts. A corporation can only act through its agents. The agents are generally the corporate officers and directors, who have contract authority. This authority may come from the corporate charter or from a resolution of the board of directors. When you deal with a corporation, you deal with its agents. Be sure to get written authority.

Agents signing for their principals must have written authority from those principals. As with corporate agents, it is always a good idea to get evidence of that written authority to avoid misunderstandings.

Partnerships are considered competent parties. Usually, the signature of one general partner is binding on the partnership; it is, however, always safer to get the signatures of all the general partners, if possible. The signature of a managing partner may be all you need. In transactions involving corporations, partnerships, or any other potentially complicated situations, it is best to seek the advice and assistance of your attorney.

Identifiable description of the premises. The legal address of the property is usually a sufficient description. If only a part of a property is being leased, you may want to describe that portion more specifically by dimension and location relative to the whole property. When in doubt, check with your attorney. Whatever description you use must clearly identify the specific space and property in question.

Consideration. Consideration is exchanging something of value. It could be barter or exchange of payment of money or promises. Exchanging promises is often the consideration in leases. An owner may promise to allow use and possession of his property in exchange for the tenant's promise to pay a specified dollar amount.

An additional consideration, especially in single family rentals may be the exchange of a specified dollar value of rent for labor. The labor might include repairs, maintenance, property improvements, or gardening. If you include such exchanges in your lease be sure you spell out the terms very specifically. For example, if proper care of the garden is a concern in your rental, it may be practical and economical for your tenant to take care of the gardening. Rather than a blanket statement knocking fifty or one hundred dollars off the rent for "gardening," detail exactly what you want done and when (for example, lawn watered daily during certain times of the year). Be as specific as you can. Your idea of "taking care of the yard" may differ considerably from your tenants. Don't take chances; spell it out. Don't assume that the tenant will love your prize roses as much as you do. Again, your attorney is the best person to help you draft unique provisions in your lease or addenda to your lease. Also, for accounting purposes, it is usually best to charge full rent, then pay the "gardener" for services completed. This keeps your income and expenses clean.

Legality of use. Any contract must have a legal purpose for it to be enforced. For example, if you rented a particular property to a tenant for use as a day care center or motorcycle repair shop and the zoning ordinances prohibited such use, your contract would be unenforceable. Most residential leases provide that the premises be used only as a residence for the tenants. The obvious intent of such a provision is to prohibit the use of the property for an unauthorized business activity, which could infringe upon the rights of neighbors or other residents of the building. This type of provision also prevents overcrowding, which might cause physical damage to the property or create health and safety problems.

Beginning and ending dates. Common law and common sense dictate that your lease indicate when it begins and when it ends. Without such a statement the lease terms are generally considered to be too vague to be enforceable.

Rights and obligations of the parties. Most of the lease contains provisions and clauses relating to the rights and obligations of the parties to the lease. The following section outlines many of these standard clauses. Some are discussed in other parts of this book in greater detail. Many are discussed in little or no detail because they vary so much from state to state as to make a general discussion useless. Some are self-explanatory.

Standard Lease Clauses

1. *Payment of rent provision.*
2. *Clause of quiet enjoyment* grants the tenant quiet and peaceful enjoyment of the property without undue interference by

the owner or his agents. This is one of the tenant's basic rights as previously discussed.

3. *Maintenance clauses* detail who is responsible for specific maintenance of the property. In residential leases, it is typically the owner who is responsible for all maintenance with the exception of tenant-caused damage.

4. *Provision requiring compliance with applicable laws.*

5. A *utility clause* details who pays for which utilities.

6. *Insurance provisions.*

7. *Alterations and improvement clause* prohibits the tenant from making unauthorized improvements and alterations.

8. A *sublet clause* prohibits the tenant from subletting or assigning his lease rights to others without written permission from the owner. This clause usually says that the owner will not unreasonably withhold his consent to assign or sublet.

9. A *"partial destruction" clause* establishes procedures in the event that the premises are damaged or destroyed by fire or other calamity. This clause usually prevents the tenant from terminating the lease because of partial destruction provided that the owner make repairs within a given time. The lease is usually terminated in the event of total destruction.

10. A *default clause* establishes rights and procedures should either party default. These rights and procedures are governed by state and local law.

11. *Hold harmless clauses* provide that the owner will not be liable for damages or injury to tenants or others on the property. They tend to appear all-inclusive, absolving the owner of all liability whether or not he is at fault or negligent. In reality, you cannot contract away responsibility for your own negligence and liability. Don't rely on the hold harmless clause as a substitute for good comprehensive liability insurance to protect your interests.

12. *Right of entry clauses* usually allow the owner to enter the premises (with reasonable notice, at reasonable times) to make inspections or repairs. Your right to enter your rental is controlled by law regardless of what your contract says.

13. A *tenancy holdover clause* establishes the terms of the tenancy when the tenant does not vacate the premises at the end of

the lease period. Typically, these clauses allow the tenant to continue the tenancy with the same terms and conditions on a month-to-month basis. Don't confuse a holdover clause with an automatic renewal clause or a delivery of possession clause.

14. A *delivery of possession clause* prevents voiding or terminating the lease and eliminates or mitigates any loss to the owner should he be unable to deliver possession of the premises on the agreed date. He may be unable to deliver due to an occupancy holdover by the previous tenant or as a result of incomplete work on the property.

15. *Bankruptcy, insolvency and receivership clauses* usually provide that the tenant's filing for bankruptcy or insolvency breaks the lease. Applicable state or federal laws control the rights of the owner in such cases.

16. A *"time is of the essence" clause* indicates that the contract conditions must be made at the precise moment specified or the contract is breached. Courts have generally determined, however, that there is no breach of contract if the contract conditions are performed within a reasonable period of time.

17. A *condemnation clause* allows that if the government takes the property (through condemnation or eminent domain) during the term of the lease, the owner is relieved of performing the balance of the contract through no fault of his own. The clause eliminates the owner's liability to the tenant due to the condemnation and terminates the lease.

18. *Automatic renewal clauses* eliminate the need for renegotiating terms of short-term leases and often allow for lease renewals with the same terms for the same period of time.

This list of possible lease provisions is not inclusive, but does cover many of the clauses that are frequently used.

The contracts used in your jurisdiction may contain variations of these clauses or may not include them at all.

Collecting Rent

Rent collection, on time, is the basis of your successful and profitable rental business. If you can't collect the rent, you may be out of business.

As mentioned previously, rents are traditionally paid in advance on the first of the month. Your rental contract needs to state that very clearly. Your tenants need to understand that policy from the very beginning of your relationship. If you don't make your rent collection policy clear, you will probably have trouble collecting the full amount on time. Don't ever let your tenants get behind in their rent payments. They have only so much to spend every month. Impress upon them that you expect payment of the rent to be their first priority.

Establishing and communicating to your tenants a practical rent-collection policy is one of the most important actions you need to take as a rental owner. Over the years, I have managed hundreds of rental units and have developed a rent-collection policy that I am comfortable with and that works for me. Here's what I do:

- During the move-in orientation (see Chapter Eight) I go over the rental agreement point by point with my new tenants. I don't assume any knowledge or understanding on their part, no matter who they are. I say aloud both the amount due and the due date, even though both have been said before.
- I then make it easy for them. I give them envelopes addressed to my office. The envelope routine may or may not be practical for you, but it works for me.
- I then let them know that if I haven't received the rent by the fifth of the month, I will be at the rental on the sixth with an eviction notice.
- I make very clear that I can accept no excuse for any late payments.
- If I have not received the rent by the fifth, I keep my word: They do get the eviction notice on the sixth.

Not everyone agrees with the policy of allowing any "grace period." I do it for two reasons: 1) Lenders do it, and 2) It allows that "reasonable period of time" for payment.

The actual payment of the rent can be by personal check, money order, cashier's check, cash, or third-party checks. Personal checks are, by far, the most practical and popular methods of payment. If I get a rent check returned marked "NSF"(not sufficient funds), my policy is that:

1. It must be replaced within a certain period of time with cash, cashier's check, or money order.
2. I consider the payment late and subject to an eviction notice until covered.

3. All future payments must be by cash, cashier's check or money order.

4. The tenant is responsible for any additional bank costs.

This policy is also made clear during the move-in orientation.

Many large apartment complexes and management firms have a "No Cash" policy because of the risk involved with large amounts of cash on hand. Cash is, however, legal tender and refusal to accept it may void the debt. Cash should never be sent by mail. Daily bank deposits reduce the risk of having cash around.

From an owner or management viewpoint, cashier's checks and money orders are the safest method of rent payment. For a tenant, they are expensive and inconvenient. As a matter of policy, they should be accepted, but not required.

Avoid third-party checks, if you can. Social Security and company payroll checks may be perfectly safe, but they usually require change and can complicate your bookkeeping.

Late Charges

There is much debate in the rental industry about the pros and cons of charging a fee if the rent payment is late. The rationale for late charges is that they encourage tenants to pay their rent on time. If you do charge a fee for the late payment of rent, be sure it is spelled out in your rental agreement. State clearly what it is and when it is to be charged. The amount of any late charge must be "reasonable" or it may be declared by the court as invalid or usurious. In some jurisdictions charging late fees may delay the eviction process and actually encourage late rent payments.

Raising Rent

Raising the rent is usually considered one of the least pleasant of the tasks you face as a rental owner. When to raise the rent, how much to raise it, and how to do it without driving your tenant away are rarely easy decisions to make. Your costs of owning and maintaining rentals go up occasionally, and so too, must your rents if you are to maintain a positive cash flow.

The best time to raise the rent is between tenants. When you have a vacancy, you can determine a realistic rent level while you do your repairs, maintenance, and cleaning. (See Chapter Eight, for some pointers). You can then advise your new tenant that you generally consider rent increases on an annual basis so that you can keep up with your increasing costs. If your tenant knows that you do raise the rent periodically, then the shock will be lessened and you have a better chance of keeping the tenant. Do not raise your rents too often or too much. Unreasonable or unjustified rent increases can only cause problems with your tenant.

How to raise the rent is governed by state law. If you have a lease, you cannot raise the rent within the lease period without an escalator clause. Normally in month-to-month rentals you must give a change of terms of tenancy notice at least 30 days prior to the increase. Allowing a little more time than the required period is a courtesy that gives your tenant more time to accept the increase and tends to lessen the impact. Once you have given proper legal notice, your tenant has two choices: 1) Stay in the unit and accept the increase, or 2) Move out.

It is always a nice touch to include a personal note with your formal notice.

Security Deposits

The subject of security deposits often causes conflict between owners of rental property and their tenants. A security deposit is a refundable deposit paid by the tenant to the owner of a rental to guarantee compliance with the terms of the rental agreement. Security deposits are governed by state law. The following is an outline of possible regulations that you need to know so as to handle your security deposits legally and fairly.

- The maximum amount chargeable may be restricted to one or two months rent.
- Usual legal deductions include rent loss, property damage, and cleaning costs. Past due utility bills might also be a legitimate deduction.
- You may need to keep the security deposit in a separate escrow or trust account.
- You may be required to pay interest on the amount.
- The unused portion of the deposit may be required to be returned within 15 or 30 days from the time the tenant moves out.
- The law may specify that all deposits are included: key deposits, pet deposits, last month's rent, etc.
- Always itemize and document any deductions.

- Many states impose penalties for violations of the security deposit regulations.

The laws regulating security deposits can be very confusing and are subject to change. Whatever the regulations are in your state, be sure to itemize and document any expenses you deduct from the security deposit. Check with your attorney or local apartment association to be sure your policies are in compliance with the law.

CHAPTER 7

Discrimination and Qualification

"Fair Housing" is the law in the United States. As an owner of rental property, you have the responsibility to be familiar with state and federal antidiscrimination laws.

Federal Fair Housing Laws

The two major pieces of federal legislation which prohibit discrimination in housing are commonly referred to as the Civil Rights Act of 1866 and the Civil Rights Act of 1968.

The Civil Rights Act of 1866 says: "All citizens of the United States shall have the same right, in every State and Territory, as is enjoyed by white citizens thereof to inherit, purchase, lease, sell, hold and convey real and personal property." On June 17, 1968, the U.S. Supreme Court held that the 1866 law prohibits "all racial discrimination, private as well as public, in the sale or rental of property."

Title VIII of the 1968 Civil Rights Act is also known as the Federal Fair Housing Law. It declares a national fair housing policy throughout the United States. This law provides that any discrimination in the sale, lease or rental of real property based on race, color, religion, sex, or national origin is prohibited. You need to know that as an owner of rental property you are required under the federal law not to discriminate in the rental of property on the basis of:

- race
- color
- religion
- sex
- national origin

Additionally, you cannot permit any real estate broker or salesperson acting as your agent to convey for you any limitations in the rental of your property based on the above. That means that you cannot quote different terms, conditions, and availability to different people. You must treat all applicants equally.

State Laws

Many states have expanded fair housing statutes that also prohibit discrimination based on:

- marital status
- physical disability
- children
- age
- arbitrary classifications

Various state courts have determined that arbitrary classifications could include:

- students
- welfare recipients
- entire occupations
- homosexuals
- non-homosexuals
- republicans
- democrats
- motorcyclists
- or who knows

Arbitrary classifications could include just about any group you could name. The point is that you must treat all rental applicants equally on the basis of objective qualifications.

Qualifying Your Applicants

As a rental property owner, you do have the right to choose the best qualified rental applicants. Your choice, however, cannot be based on illegal considerations. You have the right to do the following:

1. Screen applicants based on objective business qualifications.

2. Request a completed rental application.

3. Request references: employment, credit, banking, former landlords and personal references.

4. Establish income in relation to rent requirements; for example, income three times the amount of rent.

5. Require compliance with reasonable conditions and occupancy policies.

6. Limit the number of persons per unit.

7. Establish pet limitations or prohibitions. (Signal, service, or guide dogs may be exempt from pet provisions.)

Even some of these requirements, such as an income requirement, are being challenged in state courts. Basically, you do have the right to determine that applicants will:

- be able to pay the rent on time
- not disturb neighbors or other tenants
- maintain the rental in reasonable condition

Play it safe. Be objective. Always keep in mind that as an owner of rental property you have the responsibility to:

- Equally consider all qualified applicants.
- Show no preference in advertising or showing vacancies.
- Give all applicants complete, accurate information about terms and conditions of your rental.
- Avoid written or verbal inquiries about any applicant's race, color, religion, sex, national origin, or other classifications that have been determined by your state to be discriminatory.

It is not difficult to innocently cross the line and ask a discriminating question. Recently, I had a young couple apply for one of my vacancies. The young lady said that she had met her husband at their church youth group. I had to refrain from asking "Oh, really? Which church?"; possible grounds for a claim of religious discrimination. I urge you to be extremely cautious and objective in your conversation and language during the entire screening process.

CHAPTER 8

Ten Steps to Getting and Keeping Good Tenants

PART 1: PROPER PRIOR PLANNING

Getting and keeping good tenants who pay the rent on time and respect your property is vital to your investment. A good tenant is by far the single most important factor in your rental business. A bad or poorly selected tenant can not only wreck your property physically, but can destroy your financial security and create serious health problems as well.

Tales of Woe

Horror stories abound at property management classes, *For Rent By Owner* Seminars, and Rental Owner Courses about what poorly selected tenants can do to a unit. They have painted rooms, apartments, or entire houses colors ranging from black or olive drab to brilliant psychedelics. They have attached by glue, cement, staple, nail, or spike all manner of unremovable posters, mirrors, corkboard, or whatever to walls and ceilings. They have transformed driveways and yards into used car lots; converted closets or bathrooms into mini greenhouses, complete with assorted mold and mildew; rearranged or destroyed landscaping by a variety of bizarre methods. You name it, it's been done! Not all of it is malicious or even intentional. Often it's a result of ignorance, irresponsibility, or incompetence; not necessarily on the part of the tenant.

These examples are not meant to dissuade real estate investors. They are intended simply to point out the overwhelming need to get good tenants in order to avoid potential disasters. The best way to avoid the stress and trauma and financial costs of dealing with a bad tenant is to do everything in your power to get a good one in the first place.

There are far more potentially good tenants than bad ones. If you are very fortunate a truly great tenant might just show up, but don't count on it. Good tenants can be created.

Creating Good Tenants

Professional property managers generally agree that the way to create good tenants involves three basic rules:

1. Provide a clean, well-maintained rental space.
2. Screen and qualify your applicants thoroughly.
3. Educate yourself and your tenant.

These three basics are so important that they should be an owner/manager's credo. Keep them in mind and you will operate your rental business with a minimum of mystery, guesswork, and frustration.

The following ten steps will help you to follow those three basic principles. The first five steps involve planning and preparation. The second five steps, which are covered in the next chapter, deal directly with that prospective great tenant.

1. Know your product (your rental).
2. Know your market.
3. Determine market rent.
4. Prepare a tenant information packet.
5. Prepare the rental.
6. Advertise effectively.
7. Presentation.
8. Qualify your applicants.
9. Move-in orientation.
10. Communicate!

The implementation of each of these steps requires that you be familiar with a variety of federal, state, and local laws, ordinances, and statutes. Before you even begin these ten steps: EDUCATE YOUR-SELF!!

Step One: Know Your Product

The rental process is a marketing or sales process. While marketers or sales people may not always agree on methods or techniques (or titles), they do acknowledge that the process cannot begin until you know what you are selling (or marketing) and to whom.

What exactly is it that you are trying to rent? Start with its identity. Is it a room, a studio, an apartment, a condominium, a house, a duplex, any of the other plexes, a garage, a barn? Identify everything you can about your rental. It is a unique property and you need to be thoroughly familiar with it.

Create and complete a Property Information Sheet. You could use a 3 x 5 card, a 5 x 8 card, a single sheet of binder paper, or whatever fits your filing system. Write down everything you know (and can find out) about your rental in a logical order. The following format will help you get started, but don't limit the information you compile to this list.

PROPERTY INFORMATION SHEET

Property: (address) _____ Rent: _____

Type of Unit: _____ Deposit: _____

Location: (neighborhood, cross streets, distances to public transportation, etc.)

_____

_____

Description
Exterior Appearance: (including landscaping)

Condition: _____

Porch or Deck: _____

Patio or Yard: _____

Pool: _____

View or Special Features: _____

Available Parking: _____

Utilities: (type and estimated costs) _____

Heating/ Air Conditioning: _____

Fireplace or Woodstove: _____

Square Footage: _____

Number of Rooms: _____

Description of Rooms: (size, windows, wall and floor coverings, etc. If furnished, include inventory for each room.)

Living Room: _____

Dining Room: _____

Kitchen: _____

Bedrooms: _____

Bathrooms: _____

Family Room or Den: _____

Basement: _____

Garage: _____

Storage/Work areas: _____

Other: _____

Be meticulous. Cover everything you can possibly think of. You'll probably surprise yourself when you really start looking and writing. You should also add useful information, such as the names and locations of utility companies, churches and synagogues; libraries, community centers, parks and recreation facilities; public transportation systems and nearest stops; shopping areas; post office; emergency phone numbers; and any other information which would help you and your tenant get to know the property and the community better.

Attach to your Property Information Sheet a photograph, floor plan drawing, and area map, if you can. The more you and your tenants know about your rental and its location, the better off everyone will be. Try not to leave any gaps in your information. Be prepared to answer prospective tenant's questions about your rental. Each rental is different. Be as thorough about your product knowledge as you can be.

I remember getting an ad call on my first home rental. The woman calling asked for the name and location of the nearest elementary school. At the time, I didn't have an answer for her. She wasn't very interested in the other information I had about the rental; the double garage, the new interior paint, or the wall-to-wall carpet. All of this made it an attractive rental, but it wasn't what she needed to know. She chose not to leave her phone number, saying she would call back. She didn't, and I may have lost a good prospective tenant by not having the information that was important to her.

Everyone has different priorities when looking for a suitable rental. It's impossible to second guess your prospects' concerns and it's not worth trying. Provide complete, accurate information to all inquiries about your rental.

Step Two: Know Your Market

What is a market? What determines what rent you can charge for any given property?

A market is defined as a place where buyers and sellers meet to bargain and exchange. So, a market is comprised of both buyers and sellers. As the owner (the seller) of space available for rent, you need to know what the renters (buyers) are paying for what. The most effective and efficient way to find out is by using some form of a Market Comparison Survey. Go shopping. See for yourself. Check the newspaper and call several rentals that sound similar to yours. Drive around and see as many as you can. You'll find out soon enough what is renting and what is not, and for how much. Take scrupulous notes. (You can make up your own codes or abbreviations to save time.)

In your survey, you need to compare your rental with others on the market: location, type of unit, size, number of rooms, rental amount, security deposit, lease, appearance/appeal, age/condition, furnished or unfurnished, appliances, utilities, are pets allowed?, parking, proximity to transportation, schools, churches, shopping. Note the date of your comparison and any other comments you feel are appropriate to determine a realistic value for your rental.

This list of comparable elements is by no means inclusive. Add whatever you feel is appropriate. Your comparisons should be made with a view toward maintenance, desirability, location, and amenities. Look at each property from a renter's point of view. How do these properties compare, either positively or negatively to your property? Is the property location within each neighborhood more or less desirable than yours and why? Consider the level of maintenance of surrounding properties, the neighborhood, traffic patterns, accessibility, shopping, and availability of other services.

Real estate professionals say there are three primary considerations in choosing properties: LOCATION, LOCATION and LOCATION! One of the properties I manage in rural Northern California is a beautiful new energy efficient home on five acres with decks, three bedrooms, two baths, a big garage, and loads of amenities. However, it is very difficult to get to; a poorly maintained, steep gravel road that is barely passable or snowed in during the winter. If this home were closer to town it would command another $150 to $200 in rent. Location is a prime consideration in your comparisons.

Learn to compare your property from as many perspectives as you can so that you can be competitive and realistic in establishing your rent. Also include in your comparison survey notes information about the security deposits and rental policies. For instance, you would be at a marketing disadvantage if you set your security deposit much higher than comparable rentals. You may have perfectly valid opinions about why your rent or security deposit should be higher, but unless they are competitive, your opinions about them are worthless and counter-productive.

Knowing your market involves not only knowing the competition, but also knowing who your "customer" is: the tenant. Many people seem to think that a tenant is a second class citizen: only a renter. There need be no social stigma attached to the term "tenant." By definition a tenant is simply a person who pays rent to an owner for the right to use or occupy his property. Some of the world's wealthiest people and largest corporations are tenants. Tenants come in all shapes, sizes, sexes, colors, occupations, ages, dispositions, and personalities. They can be single or married, students or retired, quiet, loud, good, bad, or ugly. In other words, they can be just about anybody. They can, however, be grouped into two broad categories: tenants by choice and tenants by circumstance.

Tenants by choice are typically career people, empty-nesters (couples whose children have grown and left the nest), retired people, or senior citizens. They may not want the responsibilities of home ownership. They may want the freedom a rental allows. Renting is often the most economical way to live where they want.

Tenants by circumstance are people who rent because of their current circumstances. Students away at college, for instance, need temporary housing. Young families, with or without children, need a place to live until they have saved enough of a down payment to buy their own home. Others, such as military personnel or construction workers, may choose to rent housing on an interim basis. Many people moving to new areas often choose to rent while they get to know the area before purchasing.

Knowing your market requires that you learn as much as possible about the neighborhood and community in which your rental is located. It also requires that you know what your competition is and who your prospective "customers" are.

Step Three: Establishing Competitive Rents

Supply and demand

Rent is usually determined by local rental market conditions. In some cases it is determined by local rent control ordinances. Market in this case means what a reasonable tenant is willing to pay a reasonable owner for a particular space. Most of the time (rent control notwithstanding) values are determined by simple economics: supply and demand.

Supply is the total of all sellers and the quantity they are willing to sell at a given time and price. Demand is the total of all buyers and the quantity they are willing to buy at a given time and price.

For the following examples of how supply and demand work in a competitive economy, I'll use the terms "buyers" (prospective tenants, or buyers of rental space) and "sellers" (owners of rental property, or sellers of rental space).

Rental values in a market economy are determined by buyers and sellers as they compete against one another for rental space in the marketplace. Don't confuse desire or need with demand. Demand includes the ability and the willingness to spend along with desire or need. For example, Renter A wants a $750.00 a month rental, but cannot afford it. Renter B wants the same rental, can afford it, but is not willing to spend the money. Renter C wants the rental, can afford it, and is willing to spend the money. Renters A and B are "lookers," not buyers. Renter C is the only one exercising real demand for this rental. Renter C is a ready, willing, and able "buyer."

Both supply and demand in rental housing markets are subject to change. The causes of these changes are varied and complex. If you are interested in pursuing the economics of housing in more detail, I'd suggest a real estate economics course at your community college.

The demand for housing

Three primary factors influence the demand for housing: population, income, and personal taste.

Population is the most important factor influencing housing demand. After all, housing is for people; without people there is no demand for housing. It follows then, that population growth in a particular community is followed by an increase in demand for housing units. Besides numbers, another aspect of population is demographics. Demography is the population grouped according to age, sex, occupation, income level, and other variables. Demography is important because different demographic groups have different housing demands. For instance, children live with their families. Eighteen-to twenty-year-olds move into rentals. Thirty-year-olds are in more expensive rentals or are purchasing homes.

Population and demographic information is usually available from county or state planning offices, the United States Department of Housing and Urban Development (HUD), local colleges, and utility companies.

Income is the second major factor influencing housing demand. Effective demand for rental housing is created by need or desire, willingness, and ability to pay. Ability translates into income level. People who lack sufficient income cannot afford adequate housing, regardless of their need. On the other hand, increased income often allows people to leave the rental market and purchase their own homes or condominiums. In addition to income changes, the availability and cost of mortgage credit is an influence on people's ability to purchase housing and consequently affects the rental market.

The third major factor influencing rental housing demand is personal taste. Minimum shelter from the elements is our most basic requirement of housing. Our choice in style, location, and assorted amenities is influenced by our observations and experiences. As our tastes change so does our demand level.

The supply of rental housing

Housing experts and community planners use a complicated equation to determine future supplies of housing. Boiled down, it looks like this:

Future housing supply equals current housing supply less units demolished or destroyed, less units converted to other uses, plus other units converted to housing, plus new construction. It is a logical formula, but not necessarily an easy one, nor one we need to dwell on.

When determining your rental value consider the following generalities about how supply and demand affect rents.

Assuming a relatively fixed supply of rentals available at any given time and place:

- An increase in demand will reduce vacancies.
- A reduction of vacancies will increase rents.

Alternatively:

- A decrease in demand increases vacancies.
- Increasing vacancies causes rents to decline.

Assuming a relatively fixed demand by renters in any given time or place:

- An increase in supply will increase vacancies.
- Increasing vacancies will reduce rents.

When you've done a thorough market comparison survey in your area for your kind of rental, you've gotten a good grasp of supply and demand. How many units are there like yours and how many people want them at what price? Set your rent accordingly.

Rent is definitely not a function of, or even related to, your mortgage payments and other building expenses. The market does not care what your payments are. If your payments are $600 and the market dictates a $500 rent, expect $500. You may eventually get some unsuspecting and naive soul to rent your place at a higher rate, but he'll probably move when he finds a better deal.

Consider what a vacancy does to your investment. Suppose market rental value is $500 and you try to get $550. If you suffer fifteen days of vacancy because of being overpriced, you've lost $250. It would take five months at the higher rate to make up the loss of your fifteen day vacancy.

Alternatively, if you haven't done your homework you could set your rent below the market level and lose income. One of my former employers, a real estate syndicator and manager of all types of income properties, loved to buy apartment complexes that had no vacancies. To him that indicated that the rents were too low. I found that he was usually right. After a thorough market survey, he would raise the rents to their market level and put the property up for sale. He consistently doubled his equity within two years. Although the rental increases caused some vacancies and much grumbling, very few tenants moved, realizing that they were simply being shifted from paying a below market rent to paying a competitive rent. (Tenants check the market, too.) The market value principal applies to all types of rentals. Do your homework and set a rental amount that is not too high or too low. Give your tenants their money's worth, but don't give your rentals away!

Be aware of the effects of supply and demand on your local rental market. Once you've done your homework with a good comprehensive market comparison survey you'll know what rent you can expect to receive for your rental.

Step Four: Prepare A Tenant Information Packet

Now is the time to put together all the forms, documents, policy statements, house rules, and all the other information you'll need to conduct business with your prospective and actual tenants. It is very important to have all this material organized before you even get your first ad call. It is also very important to understand all the information contained in these various documents, so that you can explain it all to your applicants. I include the following in my packets:

- Rental Application
- Rental or Lease Agreement
- Move-In/Out Checklist
- Cleaning Checklist
- House Rules
- Inventories
- Addenda (e.g. Waterbed Agreement, Pet Agreement, Gardening Agreement)
- Landlord/Tenant Information
- Orientation Checklist

All of this is important in defining your relationship with your tenant. It is good business to be thorough. You should be able to get most of these forms from your local or state apartment association. Landlord/Tenant information is generally available from your State Department of Consumer Affairs, Department of Fair Housing, Housing Authority, or state consumer protection agency (see Appendix B). House rules and addenda are yours to create as needed, although samples may be available through the apartment association.

Many owners object to supplying their tenants with information about their rights. I think it is just good business for all parties in a business transaction to be fully informed about their rights and obligations. Problems generally occur as a result of ignorance, not information. Typically, state-generated Landlord/Tenant brochures not only advise tenants of their rights, but also of their responsibilities and obligations in a rental situation.

Other than collecting, studying, and understanding these various forms and documents, your most time-consuming job in preparing the packet is the creation of suitable house rules.

House Rules

There may be a subtle distinction between rules and policies, but for this discussion, I'll use the terms interchangeably.

Establish fair and reasonable house rules, designed to attract and keep good tenants and discourage poor tenants. Do this before you advertise; don't make up policies and rules as you go along. All businesses are confronted with situations that call for decisions. Well-conceived rental policies will not only help you deal with sticky situations as they arise but will also help you avoid some potential problems. Fair, reasonable, well-conceived and clearly communicated policies establish the ground rules between owner and tenant. It is up to you to set the policy that best suits your objectives.

One of my clients owned several units in a large suburban condominium project. The board of directors of the homeowners association was particularly ruthless when it came to enforcing parking regulations. The vehicles of tenants and owners alike were not only routinely ticketed and their owners fined for infractions, but many of them were towed away at their owners' expense. You can imagine how upset the tenants were, particularly if they had not been made aware of such policies. The owner of the unit is responsible to the board for the actions of his tenants in such cases. Many owners who had rentals ended up paying fines and other costs on behalf of their tenants. Some also suffered rent loss and legal problems as a result of not covering the parking restrictions in their rental guidelines. If you have condominium rentals, be especially thorough in reviewing your Bylaws and Conditions, Covenants and Restrictions (CC&R's), and letting your tenants know, in writing, what use restrictions might affect them. Your policies need to be appropriate for your particular situation and location.

The most effective way to communicate your policies to your tenants is to draw up a set of rental guidelines and house rules and make sure your tenant reads and understands them. This document is a simple explanation of all the rules, regulations, and policies of your rental property that aren't covered in your rental agreement. Most, if not all, of the information you collected for your property information card should be included in your guidelines. It should be written in plain positive language. Avoid a list of negative dictates. Number one on your list of policies should be a "Fair Housing Policy." The following is a list of other items that could be covered.

Appliances	Children
Waterbeds	Pets
Noise Levels	Occupant Limits
Parking	Security Deposit
Motorcycles	Repair & Maintenance Requests
Campers	Decorating
Auto Repairs	Rent Collection
Lease Renewal	Key Control
Move-in/Out Procedures	Emergencies
Disturbances	Complaints
Storage	Schools, Churches, Libraries, etc.
Eviction Procedure	Yard Care & Gardening
Sub-Leasing	Utilities

Some of these considerations are governed by state or federal law. Many of them are also contained in a good rental agreement. In reality, these policies, guidelines, or house rules are just an extension of a good rental agreement.

Don't hesitate to establish additional policies that work for you and your property. Remember policies are only guidelines. They are not set in stone. Review them occasionally and change them when necessary. Don't expect to anticipate every situation for which a policy might be useful or applicable. Every now and then, you'll encounter a problem that you may not have a policy for. You'll also have situations come up when you may need to bend a policy a bit or change one entirely. Usually, however, good comprehensive policies will save you the time and trouble of making frequent snap decisions. Appendix A contains a copy of some sample house rules. Check with your local apartment or rental association for rules and regulations that are appropriate for your location. Use these standard lists as a guideline and modify them for your own situation. When establishing your rental policies remember their purpose: 1) to attract good tenants and 2) to keep them by maintaining good relations, understanding, and communication.

Step Five: Preparing the Rental

Preparing a rental unit involves not only physically preparing the unit for occupancy, but also includes having your advertising, rental documents and policies complete and ready. This section, however, deals with how your rental unit looks and if it's legal.

The better your rental unit looks, the more it's worth. Have the unit ready; cleaned, safe, and repaired before you show it to prospective tenants. You'd be wasting your time showing a unit that hasn't been cleaned thoroughly or repaired properly. Prospective tenants usually have very little imagination and no trust at all when told that something will be cleaned or fixed or painted. They see only the dirty windows, leaking faucet or peeling paint. If your rental isn't ready to be moved into when you show it to prospective tenants, don't expect them to come back. Don't waste their time and yours. There are exceptions, of course, and you can probably think of a few, but don't kid yourself. Generally speaking, in almost all circumstances have your unit properly repaired, painted, decorated, cleaned, and in working order, inside and out, before you show it to prospective tenants.

Curb appeal

Try visiting a few of the better managed and maintained apartment complexes in your area to see how they do it. Even in poor rental areas you'll probably find some apartment complexes that get top market rents and are full, while others are struggling. Take a close look at the successful ones and you will usually find one thing in common: they look better, both inside and out. These properties have "curb appeal."

Curb appeal goes beyond just the architecture. Properties that have curb appeal look clean, well maintained and cared for. Have you ever driven in a residential neighborhood, noticed a shabby house and thought that it must be a rental? If it is, you can bet that the owner is not getting maximum rents or the best tenants.

If you want your rental to attract better prospects, you have to prepare your product. Make it as attractive as you possibly can. Imagine two rental houses across the street from each other. Both are identical: same shape, same floor plan, same lot size, same amenities and so forth. One has curb appeal, is well maintained, landscaped, painted, clean, and looks good. The other is overgrown, shabby, and does not appear to be cared for. Both are "For Rent By Owner." The better looking house (or duplex or whatever) will attract more qualified prospects, rent faster at a higher rate, have fewer tenant problems, less maintenance problems, and generally be a more satisfying business venture. Remember that your job as a rental property owner is to rent your unit at the best possible rent to the best possible tenant.

Take a thorough, critical objective tour of your own property to see how it might be improved and cleaned up to attract better tenants and get more rent. The chapter on maintenance will help you identify and correct specific problems.

Safety

Beyond making your rental look good, you'll need to comply with the Health and Safety Codes for rental housing of your state or locality. Most of these regulations include a list of conditions that are considered to endanger the life, limb, health, property, safety, or welfare of the public or the occupants of rentals. The wording is different from state to state but many include the following list of conditions that are considered substandard.

1. Inadequate sanitation, including, but not necessarily limited to, lack of, or improper:
   - bathtub or shower
   - kitchen sink
   - hot and cold running water
   - heating
   - ventilating equipment
   - electrical lighting
   - dampness
   - infestation of insects, vermin, or rodents
   - general dilapidation
   - improper maintenance
   - sewage disposal system
   - garbage storage and removal

2. Structural hazards, including, but not necessarily limited to the following areas:
   - foundations
   - flooring or floor supports

- walls and other vertical supports
- ceilings and roofs
- fireplaces or chimneys

3. Any nuisance
4. All wiring
5. All plumbing
6. All mechanical equipment
7. Water protection including:
   - plaster
   - waterproofing/paint, etc.
   - doors and windows
   - wall coverings and roof coverings
8. Fire hazards
9. Construction materials
10. Inadequate maintenance
11. Compliance with Uniform Building Code
12. Fire extinguishing systems, etc.

That's a long list. Not all jurisdictions include all of these items. Check with the appropriate agency in your locality or with the local apartment or owners' associations for the specific regulations. Your concept of what is healthy and safe may differ from the government's. Be aware that there could be stiff penalties and serious liabilities involved in what the government considers substandard housing, especially rental housing.

Painting and cleaning

The benefits of painting some or all of your rental interior far outweigh the cost and effort. New paint not only looks great, but smells great, and shows your prospects the level of care you've given your unit (and expect it to receive from them).

Prepare a cleaning checklist. You can use this list both in preparing your rental for a new tenant and for your tenant to use when moving out. The cleaning checklist is a companion document to the Move-in/Out Checklist. Appendix A contains an example of a good, thorough cleaning checklist.

Don't be content to just vacuum your carpets. Renting a commercial shampooer from the supermarket is not only cost effective, but again shows your prospects your level of commitment.

Are you ready?

The following list will help you to determine if your rental is ready to be shown:

- Walls and ceilings are freshly painted. (Don't forget closets and shelves.)
- Carpeting is vacuumed and shampooed. (Burned or stained areas have been repaired or replaced.)
- All windows were washed inside and out.
- Window sills, sashes, ledges, and shelves are wiped clean.
- All lights work; fixtures and switches are washed.
- All floors are washed, waxed, and shining.
- All kitchen appliances are spotless and in working order. (Don't forget the under-sink cabinet, under the burners on the stove, and the refrigerator door gaskets.)
- All bathrooms are spotless; no drips or stains.
- All leftovers have been removed: coat hangers, used soap, razor blades, cleaning supplies, toilet paper.

Many apartment complexes post the checked-off checklist as testimony to the readiness of the unit; a nice touch. I'd also recommend a final inspection just before showing the rental to your prospects.

Now your rental property is prepared for renters. You've completed the first five steps of the ten steps to getting and keeping great tenants. The next chapter tells you how to start the people phase of getting those great tenants.

CHAPTER 9

Ten Steps to Getting and Keeping Good Tenants

PART 2: THE PEOPLE PROCESS

Step Six: Effective Advertising

Getting a good tenant involves a selling process. As owner or manager of rental property, you are selling rental space. The prospective tenants wish to sell their qualifications to you. There are four steps in the selling process. Whenever you buy anything you go through these steps:

1. Attention
2. Interest
3. Desire
4. Action

Most typical sales follow those steps. Advertising rentals can include the first two or three steps. The steps are based on good psychology. They make good sense and you need to be aware of them when you advertise. Unless you get a prospective tenant's attention, he or she has nothing to be interested in. A prospect becomes interested if there is reason to believe that your unit offers benefits: size, location, amenities, cost, and any other considerations the prospect may have. Most often desire is a matter of letting your prospect be convinced that your place is right rather than doing the convincing yourself. Action is signing the lease or rental agreements and exchanging money and moving in.

Remember: this process has a flip side. The prospect has to get your attention, interest, and desire as a suitable tenant and get you to take positive action toward his or her application. More on that side of the coin later.

How can your advertising get a prospective tenants' attention? Advertising itself can take many forms. It can encompass everything from word of mouth to flyers, posted cards, signs, and newspaper ads. Your advertising campaign needs to lead prospective tenants through the four steps effectively or at least get them started. The primary goal of your advertising is to attract as many qualified prospective tenants as possible.

Current tenant

The least expensive method of seeking a qualified tenant is to ask your current tenant if he or she knows anyone who might be interested in the rental after they leave. Needless to say, you don't do that if you are dissatisfied with your current tenant. In a tight rental market where the supply is low and the demand high, that may be all you need to do.

Posted notices

The next least expensive method is to place 3 x 5 cards on bulletin boards in strategic locations and For Rent signs on the property itself. Depending on your situation and the type of tenant you seek, consider the following possible locations for cards:

- where you work
- churches, synagogues
- colleges, universities
- libraries
- community centers
- shopping centers/grocery stores
- restaurants
- bookstores
- laundromats
- military bases

Your card needs to be worded so as to attract the attention of prospective tenants. It basically needs to tell prospects WHAT, WHERE, and HOW MUCH. Consider the following examples.

✦

FOR RENT BY OWNER 2/10/93
STUDIO APARTMENT

- $500 per month ($750 Deposit [refundable])
- Utilities included
- 2 blocks from Senior Citizens Center
- Available 3/1/93
- No Pets
- Furnished or Unfurnished
- Prefer Nonsmoker

Call (123) 987-6543

✦

FOR RENT BY OWNER
2/10/93
3 BR. 2 BA. HOME DRY CREEK AREA

* On 5 acres   * $1250 per month
* Family room   * Double garage
* Garden area   * Storage
* Fireplace   * Woodstove
* Deck   * Barn
* Lease/purchase option

Call (321)345-6789

✦

You can't say everything there is to say about your rental on a 3 x 5 card. Keep in mind that this first advertising step is designed to get attention and interest. Since they are attention-getting devices, give some thought about where to place your cards.

"For Rent" signs on property
You can buy For Rent signs at most hardware stores and many of the larger supermarkets. Your sign should be clean, visible, and read-

able. The phone number should be written clearly with a waterproof marker and be legible from the street. This sign is strictly an attention getter for passing motorists and pedestrians so it needs to be placed where it will get attention. It will do you no good stuck in a window where people passing by won't be able to see it. Some cities and condominium communities have placed restrictions on the use and placement of such signs, so be sure it's legal first. As a courtesy to your existing tenants, if any, also post a "Do Not Disturb Tenants" sign.

Newspaper ads

Newspaper line ads are very cost-effective considering the number of people they reach. They target your market very precisely.

It is important for any advertising to be as specific as possible without being too wordy. A well written ad (in whatever form: card, newspaper, etc.) will save you a lot of wasted time in dealing with prospects who might not be interested in what you have to offer, or who might not qualify. Your ads need to be clear, concise, and informative.

The people who work in the classified department of your local newspaper can help you structure an effective ad. You should know what you want to say. Ask for their help in preparing an ad. They usually know what gets attention and what does not. They also know how to keep the ad simple. Today, after writing hundreds of line and display ads, I still ask the newspaper advertising representative for his or her opinion, suggestions, and advice. The representative usually knows which ads work and which do not. It's their job to know.

When you place your line ad in the newspaper, ask about reduced rates. Most newspapers offer discounts for certain time periods (for example, a seven-day rate as opposed to a daily rate). Check to see what works best for your market area. Be sure to ask about the terms of cancellation. Note the cancellation procedure and the phone number. There are two occasions to cancel your ad: 1) when it has worked and, 2) when it isn't working. If you get a satisfactory tenant, qualified, signed, and paid, cancel the ad. If you don't get enough qualified callers from your ad, cancel it, then write and place another one as quickly as possible.

Handling telephoned responses to your ad

A well-written ad should bring phone calls, depending, of course, on your local market situation—supply and demand for your type of unit at your price. If you've done your homework you will get calls.

Before the phone rings have the following available near the phone:

1. Property Information Sheet
2. Tenant Information Packet
3. Copy of ad
4. Area map
5. Pad and pencil
6. Prospective tenant log

When interested parties do call, many will want to know the address right away. As long as they are clear on the terms, conditions, tenant qualifications and description of the rental, there is no reason not to tell them.

In order to eliminate wasted time and effort, I would strongly encourage owners of rental properties to state the terms of the rental agreements clearly. Describe the property and rental conditions as completely as you can. Now is the time to use the Property Information Sheet that you so carefully completed. Full disclosure has its rewards. There is never any value in letting tenants find out negative aspects of the place for themselves after they move in. (Oh! Did I forget to tell you that the house was haunted?) Don't withhold any information about the property or about your rental policies. You don't need to read your policy statement or house rules verbatim, but do advise prospects of items that may affect their eligibility: your tenant qualifications.

Do give prospects the opportunity to drive by and check the rental on their own. Telling the location of your rental is not a commitment on your part to rent on a first-come, first-served basis. In a tight rental market, some callers may want you to commit to renting to them. Don't even be tempted. By giving the location to callers who may qualify you are merely moving the selling process along from interest to desire.

You should make very clear to callers that current tenants should not be disturbed. Should someone ignore this request don't hesitate to cross them off your prospective applicant list. The more prospective applicants who view the rental at this point, the better your odds for selecting a qualified responsible tenant. This initial drive-by serves two essential functions. It further screens or qualifies prospects by allowing you to determine how responsible they are in following instructions. It also allows them to screen the property for themselves. It may not be suitable for them for a variety of reasons and they won't take up any more of your time.

By being open and honest about both the positive and negative aspects of your rental, you will achieve three positive results. First, callers will appreciate your honesty and will tend to conduct any future dealings with you accordingly. Second, when prospects do look at the property they will be prepared for the worst. Quite often they will assure you that what you perceived as a problem area is not a major concern for them. Third, if a caller needs something other than what you have to offer, very little time will have been wasted by either party.

Your telephone voice and attitude when answering ad calls have an effect on the caller. Remember: you will be entering into a business relationship with at least one of the callers. Your local telephone company has a booklet on the subject of answering telephones that is loaded with helpful information. Some of the highlights include:

1. Listen to what the caller is asking and saying.
2. Express interest in the caller.
3. Use simple, plain, everyday language.
4. Speak clearly and distinctly; talk directly into the mouthpiece.
5. Use a normal tone of voice; not too loud or soft, fast or slow.
6. Be polite, friendly, and courteous; don't hesitate to use please, thank you, and you're welcome.

Everyone has his or her own personality. You don't need to be phony. When you can't be there to answer the calls yourself, you'll need someone intelligent and old enough to give all the pertinent information clearly and accurately. You might also consider using a telephone answering machine.

Telephone answering machines are more than a matter of convenience, especially when you are handling your own rental calls. Without one you have two choices: 1) having someone available constantly to answer the phone, or 2) missing important calls. In your rental business, neither of these options is practical. With an answering machine you can schedule return calls at your convenience.

The recorded message should be clear and concise. How many times have you hung up on a machine? Keep your message simple. When the property is definitely rented (tenant qualified and paid up) say so. When the property is still available, say so and request the caller's name and number. Let the caller know approximately what time he or she can expect your return call; then call!

Prospective tenant log

Keep track of your callers on a single sheet of paper, not on scraps. Your log might look something like this:

———————— ✦ ————————

PROSPECTIVE TENANT LOG

FOR: 7001 BERMAN STREET

Date/Time	Name	Home#	Work#	Comments
2/16 8am	Fred Zool	731-1371		Married; 7 kids; 3 dogs; uncounted cats; a Boa; a gerbil; unemployed
2/16 9:15am	Rhoda Fuss	731-1111		single, exec. sec. income $2,500/mo; will drive by
2/16 9:30am	Harry Kishner	731-0001	(message)	single; extended family; "spiritual counselor," will dance by

———————— ✦ ————————

In the comments column, jot down whatever you feel is pertinent. Include your impression of the caller as well as facts they may give you. Be sure to put down only facts that relate to the rental and qualifying. There is sometimes a fine line between illegal discrimination and legal qualifying. Your comments should not include things like "has accent" or "sounds gay" or anything else that might constitute discrimination.

Step Seven: Presentation

The dictionary defines presentation as the act of presenting. Presenting means to bring before someone; to bring to view or notice; to display; to exhibit; to submit for consideration. The presentation of your rental property definitely includes all of that. Part of your presentation is covered by your advertising. The way you answer your telephone calls and conduct your business are also important parts of your presentation.

The only reason I'm making a distinction between the overall advertising and presentation is to point out the importance of your role as the presenter. Your attitude and "presentation" may make the difference between mediocre and great renters. Very often tenants reflect your attitude and commitment to providing a quality service. We all have a tendency to return what we get. If you give fair, equitable and honest service and value, your tenant's treatment of you and your property will reflect that. When you think about it these steps to getting a great tenant are a reflection of the quality of your presentation.

Showing your rental

The "presentation" of your property is on the line when you actually show the rental to prospective tenants. After your preliminary telephone screening of the callers, and after they have driven by and are interested, they will call for an appointment to see the inside. Schedule appointments at least one-half hour to forty-five minutes apart to allow a leisurely and thorough viewing. This allows plenty of time for all the parties involved to size each other up. This also allows enough time for questions, answers, and applications, if appropriate. One of the main problem areas in the screening process is not allowing enough time to show the rental properly and communicate with the prospects. Listen to what they are saying and how they say it.

In showing the rental unit try not to hover over your prospects. Give them some space. Be calm. Don't give the impression that you're willing to accept the first offer that comes by. Be available to answer questions. When you don't have an answer, say so. Point out features that might not be obvious. Your prospects know what bedrooms and bathrooms look like. They might not be aware of the abundance of storage space, large hot water heater, high-grade carpeting, or number of electrical outlets.

Atmosphere

The atmosphere you've created in preparing your unit can make a big difference. I highly recommend that you turn up the air conditioner (or open windows) in the summer; turn on the heat in the winter to create a comfortable environment. Also, turn on the lights and open the drapes for full light. Consider the contrast between showing a cold unit and telling prospects that the heater really does work and viewing a warm, cozy, comfortable residence. It is also a good idea to use a pine or floral room deodorizer. Do everything you can to make the unit clean, bright, fresh, and appealing. Remember the old adage, "Actions speak louder than words." Do everything you can to generate desire.

The close

The final step in the selling process is what professional sales people call *the close*: Ask the prospect if they'd like to fill out a rental application. This takes them from desire to action. It is important that you offer applications to all of your prospects who are interested. If you don't you may be illegally discriminating whether you are aware of it or not.

Step Eight: Screening and Qualifying Your Applicants

At this point you should have your rental guidelines already established and in writing. In qualifying your tenants you need to be particularly careful about discrimination. Make sure you understand and are in compliance with local, state, and federal ordinances and statutes. Review Chapter Seven, Discrimination and Qualification. Know the rules of the game. It's not difficult to get tripped up here.

Rental application

The rental application (see sample in Appendix A) is one of the most important documents that you have available to you. There are dozens of application forms available from a variety of outlets. Make sure the one you use is legal and up to date. You could be penalized if your application asks illegal questions. For example, some states prohibit asking applicants their marital status or their age. The local branch of your state apartment association is the best source for all rental documents. The local Board of Realtors also has good up-to-date forms. Avoid stationery store forms as they are often outdated and illegal.

Insist that every adult applicant who will be living in the rental complete and sign an application. Whatever form you do use should include the following key elements:

- names of prospective occupants
- present landlord
- previous landlord
- Social Security number
- driver's license number
- employment record
- credit references

- banking references
- personal references
- permission to verify information
- certification of information

The application must be signed before you can do any screening. Remember that the notes you take on information received in your screening process can be used either for or against you should a question of discrimination arise. Again, as in your telephone log, avoid notations that could be construed as discriminatory.

Holding deposits and application fees

At the time of taking the application, two questions involving money might arise. One involves a holding deposit and the other an application fee. Both of these are distinguished from the actual security deposit (see Chapter Six, All About Rents and Deposits). There are two schools of thought on holding deposits. The idea of a holding deposit is to get money from your applicants as a "show of good faith" or to insure that they are seriously interested in your rental. When you do use this type of deposit, be sure to agree in writing on terms specifying whether any portion is nonrefundable, as well as any other conditions. Many experienced landlords and managers feel that a holding deposit is more trouble than it's worth.

Another consideration is an application fee. This fee is charged to cover the costs of screening the applicant. It is usually $20.00 or more and typically offsets the fee charged for a credit check. This fee is not part of the security deposit or the rent. Since this charge is not a deposit the fee is nonrefundable and a separate receipt should be written. If you feel charging such a fee is appropriate, use it with all applicants. Again, avoid potential discrimination accusations.

The screening process

Poorly selected or improperly screened tenants can cause a variety of headaches you can do without (see the film "Pacific Heights" for some of the possibilities). Story Time:

Mr. H. a city fireman, just getting started building his real estate empire, owned two single-family rental units in a popular suburban area. He had a vacancy in one. Wanting to avoid the income loss, he quickly rented to the first likely prospect who answered his newspaper ad. The prospect seemed like a nice enough guy who had plenty of cash and drove a decent car. Mr. H., went through the motions of having the applicant fill out a rental application, but did not bother to verify any of the information: no income verification, no previous landlords . . . nothing. After all, the information on the application all looked good, and Mr. Nice Guy wanted to move in right away. No vacancy problem. Mr. Nice Guy paid Mr. H. one month's rent in cash (fortunately) and agreed to pay a security deposit with the next month's rent. See anything wrong with this picture so far? You bet! That first month's rent in cash was the first, last, and only money Mr. H. ever got from Mr. Nice Guy. After the check for the second month's rent and security deposit bounced, it took Mr. H. three weeks to catch Mr. No Good home. Then, he accepted a plausible story and a second check, which also bounced. To make a long, sad story a short, sad story, it took Mr. H. eight months, several thousands of dollars in attorney fees, and thousands of dollars in rent loss before he was finally able to evict Mr. N.G. Another hefty chunk of change, and time, was needed for repairing the damage and cleaning the rental. Even though he had a judgement from the court, Mr. H. was not able to collect one dime from his former, hastily selected tenant, who skipped town without a trace. The whole experience definitely set Mr. H.'s grand retirement plan back a few pegs. It also gave him an education he could have gotten a lot cheaper some other way (books, classes, seminars, membership in the local apartment association). Variations of this story are not uncommon across the country. You've probably heard a few yourself.

Another story: Mrs. W., a widow, did not fare so badly financially. Her experience with her tenant, who used abusive language and verbal threats, caused her severe stomach disorders. She got to the point where she would get physically ill just anticipating the phone call to ask for the delinquent rent. The rent was always paid . . . late . . . after a lot of aggravation. Her physician eventually recommended she seek professional psychological counselling, which led her to sell the property at a discount and invest in low yield securities. And she lived happily ever after.

The purpose of screening your applicants thoroughly is to determine if they would make suitable tenants. Would you consider turning over to a stranger the keys to your $25,000 automobile? Of course not. Putting it in perspective, does it not seem to you terribly irresponsible to give the keys to property worth many times the value of your automobile to a person you know very little about? Strange as it seems many owners do just that with very little thought about the consequences. Your screening needs to determine three very important things about your applicant:

1. stability
2. responsibility to care for the property
3. ability to pay the rent (on time)

If, after your screening, you are not completely satisfied about those three qualities, don't rent to that prospect.

Getting credit reports and checking references can be a tricky business. Tread carefully. You must have the applicant's written permission before you can run a credit check. Credit reports are confidential. State laws, as well as the Federal Fair Credit Reporting Act, prohibit you from disclosing any credit information obtained to anyone, including the applicants. Because of this, in order to protect both property owner and prospective tenant, many apartment associations will not usually give a written report to the owner. When you do reject an applicant because of a negative report, say only that the report was negative. Do not disclose actual credit information. Do advise the person of the name, address, and telephone number of the credit reporting agency.

Telephoning the applicant's employer to verify salary and employment record can be either a simple or complicated process depending on the size of the company. You may end up talking to someone who knows the applicant well or not at all. Don't get discouraged. Keep at it until you get the information you need. You need the following information:

- length of time on the job
- income verification
- employment stability

Try to get an objective recommendation from a supervisor who knows the applicant personally, if you can.

When checking with previous landlords you need to know what kind of tenant the applicant has been. Some applicants such as first time renters or people who owned their homes will not have previous landlords. In all other situations, however, determine the following information:

- length of time in the rental
- was rent paid on time
- did tenant take care of the rental
- reason for tenant leaving

- was proper notice given
- did tenant abide by house rules

Here's the clincher: ask the owner or manager if he would rent to this person again.

Helpful hints

1. Reports from previous landlords are more revealing than current ones. The current landlord may tell you anything to get rid of undesirable tenants, whereas previous landlords have nothing to lose by being honest.

2. Ask only questions that pertain to the rental agreement; for example, whether the prospect pays the rent on time, respects the property, and abides by the house rules.

3. When checking bank references you need to know whether the applicant has open accounts and what their ratings are. You do not need to know balances and banks will not tell you.

4. Get some sort of income verification from the applicant: paycheck stub, tax return, year-to-date statement, or anything else that proves the income.

5. It may sound silly, but do verify identification by actually looking at the applicant's driver's license, military I.D. card, passport, or state identification card. When possible, check out the applicant's car and current residence. The condition of each can tell you a lot about the applicant and how he or she takes care of things.

6. Check and verify all information carefully and thoroughly until you are completely satisfied.

The reason for qualifying your applicant is simply to find out his or her ability to pay the rent on time and respect your property. It makes zero difference if he or she is black, white, blue, gay, straight, tall, short, fat, married, ugly, or anything else. As I have mentioned before, treat all applicants equally and you'll save yourself a lot of potential problems. Keep it simple; keep it legal. There are no shortcuts in the screening process. *Thoroughly screening your applicant is the most important step in getting a good reliable tenant.* Don't take chances with your investment.

Step Nine: Move-in Procedure

Accepting the applicant

Once you have verified the information on the application and are satisfied, call your prospective tenant and say that you have accepted his or her application. If the prospect is definitely interested in your rental at this time arrange a move-in orientation meeting at the residence if possible. I allow one hour for this meeting and insist that all prospective tenants be there. The rapport that you establish with your prospective tenant during the orientation will set the stage for future interaction, attitudes and behavior patterns towards both you and your rental.

Call any other applicants you may have, tell them that you have selected a tenant and thank them for their application. Do not tell them that you are rejecting their applications. This can be treacherous. Keep it on a positive note and be sure that you can back up your choice legally if you have to.

Move-in orientation

There are two separate and important parts to a move-in procedure. One is the orientation you scheduled with your applicants and the second is a move-in inspection of the rental by your tenants. Both of these steps are intended to create a thorough understanding between owner or manager and tenant.

Of the ten steps outlined, there may be some that you might want to skip over or modify, but do *not* skip over this most important step of educating your applicant. Without a tenant who can pay the rent and understand the rules you're asking for trouble. There are several things that need to be accomplished during the move-in orientation. Take the time to ensure that they get done.

1. Review in detail the rental agreements, house rules, addenda, and inventories.
2. Have all parties sign all documents; initial specific clauses you want to emphasize.
3. Collect at least one month's rent and security deposit. (Give a receipt.)
4. Give keys. (Get receipt.)
5. Review and establish timing for move-in inspection.
6. Establish communication procedure.

This one-hour meeting is the most important block of time you will ever spend with your tenant. Treat it as you would a meeting with your accountant or attorney. Avoid all distractions, such as children, if possible.

Rental agreement

First things first: the rental agreement or lease. Since I am not an attorney and this book is written for a national readership, I am not in a position to discuss pros, cons, and legalities of all the clauses that could be in a rental agreement or lease. Again, the best source for your documents, to insure that they are up to date and legal, is your state or local apartment owners association or Board of Realtors. The best forms are often the simplest. I've seen commercial leases that run up to thirty pages, plus addenda, and require an attorney's interpretation. In most jurisdictions, an effective residential rental agreement can fit on both sides of one sheet. Regardless of how simple or complicated the form you use, make sure the following basics are included:

- date
- parties involved
- legal address of unit
- rent amount and when due
- late charge provisions, if any
- date tenancy begins
- termination of tenancy provisions
- hold over provision
- provision naming occupants
- clause or addendum covering pets
- clause about legal use of premises
- clause about decorating, altering, or repairing the premises
- determination of who pays for utilities and services
- jointly and severally liable provision
- security deposit and use provision
- attorney's fees and costs provision
- legal service clause
- subletting clause
- acknowledgment of house rules, inventories, or addenda
- signatures of owner or agent and all residents (of age)

Some of these provisions and clauses vary from jurisdiction to jurisdiction. Although some of the older, outdated forms contain illegal provisions, a tenant cannot sign away his legal rights. Whatever provisions are in your rental agreement, read each aloud and make sure that both you and your tenants understand them. In addition to the rental agreement, reach an agreement and understanding of your house rules, inventories, and addenda. These, of course, vary considerably from owner to owner and unit to unit.

Move-in/out condition report

There is one other form that deserves individual consideration and attention—the move-in/out condition report. This report goes by different names and comes in many formats. Sample forms 9 and 10 in Appendix A are good examples. The purpose of the report is to provide documentation as to the condition of the rental at the time of move-in. Don't make the mistake of letting yourself or your tenant take this for granted. There are probably more disputes and misunderstandings over the return of the security deposit than any other single issue. Impress upon yourself and your tenant that the return of any security deposit is directly related to the condition of the unit before and after the tenancy. This report is documentation of that condition.

The concept behind the use of a move-in condition report is to allow your tenant to inspect the unit thoroughly and note any damage or cleaning problems. Impress upon your tenant that any cleaning needed and/or damage not noted on the report will be their responsibility to correct or pay for when they have moved out. Normal wear and tear is not included. The inspection needs to be made and the report returned to you immediately *before* actual move-in.

As with many issues concerning property management there are a variety of opinions and policies about the move-in inspection. Some owners and managers insist on being present during the inspection of the unit by the tenant. Others have found this practice to be overly time consuming and self-defeating. I've seen cases where the tenant has successfully argued in court that the presence of the owner or manager during the inspection was distracting and caused them to overlook some existing damage for which they were being charged. On the other hand, you must rely on your tenant to be thorough and conscientious enough to return the report to you before they bang up the walls moving furniture in. It is important that you have an understanding with your tenant of the agreements and consequences as stated on the report.

Landlord/ tenant information

I recommend providing your tenant with information about the legalities of the landlord/tenant relationship. Many state apartment associations have available a pamphlet outlining rights and responsibilities under the law. The California Apartment Association, for example, provides a very concise outline entitled "Owner-Resident Rental Pamphlet" that contains an excellent summary of a complicated subject. To quote from that pamphlet:

- Misunderstandings between management and residents do occur. Usually this can be attributable to lack of knowledge regarding the rights of both parties.
- The desire to inform both owner and renter led to the creation of this pamphlet by the California Apartment Association.
- Distribution of the pamphlet is done through local association chapters. The owner of this rental is concerned or you would not have been given this for your information and protection.
- The owner must have responsible residents who pay their rent and respect the property and the rights of other residents.
- The resident must have a responsible owner who respects the renter, and provides a clean, secure, well-maintained building.
- No law can be written to cover all aspects of the rental relationship, but common sense and cooperation will resolve most disagreements.

The pamphlet covers in a paragraph or two the following subjects:

- application to rent
- discrimination
- agreements
- security deposits
- change of terms
- termination
- right to enter
- maintenance
- repair and deduct
- insurance
- resident responsibilities

The pamphlet also advises its readers that it "is not intended to be comprehensive or to give all the rights and duties of the parties in each instance."

Most state associations have this type of information available. If not, lobby them to create something. Having this information and making it available to your tenant is a clear statement of your intent and commitment about your rental business.

The California Department of Consumer Affairs publishes a brochure entitled "Landlord-Tenant: Answers to Tenant Questions." Many states have similar material that is generally available free of charge. State consumer protection agencies are listed in Appendix B. The California brochure asks and answers the following questions:

1. Can I get my deposit back?
2. If I give the landlord a deposit to hold an apartment and one of us changes his/her mind—can I get my money back?
3. How much notice do I have to give when I decide to move?
4. If repairs are needed, what should I do?
5. Can I be forced to move?
6. Can my rent be raised?
7. Can I get interest on my deposit?
8. Can my landlord enter my apartment without my permission?
9. Can I sublet my apartment to another tenant?
10. Can a landlord discriminate against certain kinds of tenants?

Can you answer all those questions? If not, get yourself educated about your state's landlord-tenant laws. I don't go over all that information with my tenants, but I do give them the material, advise them to read it, have them initial my move-in checklist that they have received it, and urge them to call me if they have any questions or problems regarding their tenancy.

Now comes the good part.

Collect the rent

After you've agreed and signed your documentation you need to collect the rent and security deposit. Both amounts have already been established and agreed upon at this point. Don't accept any less than one full month's rent. Even when the established move-in date is mid-month, it is far better to pro-rate the second month's rent than to get a partial rent up front. For example, if the rent is $750 per month and the move-in date is the fifteenth of the month and the rent is due on the first, collect $750 and make $375 due on the first of the following month. The due date can be any day you agree upon. Also, you can collect more than one month's rent in advance.

To arrive at the daily rent for purposes of pro-rating simply divide the monthly rent by thirty (regardless of how many days there are in that particular month). Example:

$$\frac{monthly\ rent}{30} = daily\ rent$$

$$\frac{\$750}{30} = \$25.00\ per\ day$$

If the move-in date is within ten days of the first of the month (and the rent is due on the first), try to get however many days rent there are plus the full months rent. Example:

Move in: May 20th
Rent Amount: $750 per month

Since June has 30 days, there are eleven days from June 20 *through* June 30

11 days x $25 per day = $275.00

The "through" versus "to" distinction could be an important one for your receipts and recordkeeping. "Through" the 30th includes the 30th; "to" the first, does not include the first.

If it is not realistic to collect the additional $275.00, collect the $750.00 for one full month and make the $275 due June 1 (not June 21). This can be confusing if you are not clear on the procedure. Remember the whole purpose of the move-in orientation is to avoid confusion and potential conflict.

As discussed in Chapter Six, your maximum security deposit is limited by state law and market conditions. You can choose to collect the whole amount or pro-rate it, depending on the market and your policies. Should you pro-rate the security deposit you must make that concession available to all applicants and not discriminate.

Now you have collected the rent and security deposit and have given a receipt for each. When you use only one receipt for both items, be sure to indicate clearly the amounts paid for each to avoid any conflict later on. You have also reviewed all documentation and have a complete understanding with your tenant of the conditions of the rental. All documents have been signed.

Move-in checklist

It's always a good idea to double check yourself to be sure you've got all the move-in procedures covered. An informal control form covering the following points could be invaluable.

Property: _____

Date vacated: _____

Utilities transferred to owner: _____

Repairs/maint. complete: _____

Drapes: _____

Carpets: _____

Cleaning: _____

Ads: _____

Showing: _____

Application received: _____

Income verified: _____

Previous residency verified: _____

App. approved/notification: _____

Move-in orientation: _____

Rent agreement: _____

House rules: _____

Addenda: _____

L/T info: _____

Security deposit: _____

One mo. rent: _____

Keys: _____

Condition report returned: _____

Utilities transferred:(to tenant) _____

Move-in date: _____

Step Ten: Communicate!

Effective communication affects both our personal and professional lives. Like the other language arts of reading and writing it requires some disciplined study. Most of us tend to be poor communicators. Most of us do not make a conscious effort to develop our communication skills. Most of us tend to distort what we see and hear. We do not listen. We can't wait to say our piece. In operating your rental business these tendencies could have disastrous results.

One of the main complaints tenants have about owner/managers or management companies is the lack of response to problems. According to Betty Gwiazdon, executive director of the Sacramento Valley Apartment Association, lack of response to maintenance requests causes more tenant problems and "turn-overs" (move-outs) than any other single issue.

Look at service requests as opportunities to further good owner/tenant relations. They can also be viewed as favors to you as the owner. Many requests ultimately reduce maintenance costs. Encourage your tenants to advise you of needed repairs.

Sometimes the situation makes it impossible to respond to a tenant's requests as quickly or in the manner the tenant would like. You should, however, let your tenants know that you are available and will make whatever arrangements are necessary as quickly as possible.

Put it in writing

Some communications need to be in writing. Eviction notices and changes in terms of tenancy such as rent increases, need to be in writing. Also be sure to make notations regarding maintenance requests and dates of completion of these requests (see recordkeeping and maintenance).

R.S.V.P

In reality each of these ten steps is a way of communicating to your prospects and tenants about your commitment and intentions as an owner of rental property. *If you want a great tenant be a great manager!* If you want responsive and responsible tenants be a responsive and responsible manager.

CHAPTER 10

Ending the Tenancy

Tenancies end either voluntarily or involuntarily. Voluntary terminations are usually not a problem. Involuntary terminations can end up with an eviction process and may be expensive and very frustrating.

Voluntary Terminations

End of lease term

A voluntary termination occurs when the tenants lease period is up and he moves. The tenant is usually not required to give notice under the terms of the lease. If the tenant wants to stay after the lease period is up, the tenant must request and receive permission from the owner and renegotiate the lease terms. If the lease has an automatic renewal provision, the tenant needs to notify the owner of his wish to stay. Even though no notice is required, it is always best to check with your tenant to determine his intentions.

30-day notice given to owner by tenant

If the tenant is on a month-to-month rental agreement, the tenant needs to give the owner proper legal notice of his intent to vacate (see form #15 in Appendix A). If the tenant does not give the required notice, he may be liable for additional rent. Impress upon your tenant during the orientation meeting that the notice to vacate needs to be in writing. The main reasons for the written notice are:

- It is written documentation of the tenant's intended move-out date.
- It protects the owner should the tenant not move out when promised.

If the owner has rented to someone else based on the written notice and the old tenant either decides to stay or is late moving, the written notice at least shows that the owner was acting in good faith. If a new tenant is unable to move in on the date promised as a result of the actions of the previous tenant, he may incur expenses and expect the owner to pay them. The written notice will help in the owner's defense should it be necessary.

Because of the potential for this type of complication, it might be a good idea to wait until the tenant has actually moved before promising the new tenant a move-in date. Waiting also gives you enough time to complete any necessary repairs, improvements, or cleaning.

Returning the security deposit
Several things need to be done immediately after the move out:

1. Get all keys returned.
2. Inspect the rental thoroughly to determine any security deposit deductions.
3. Get a forwarding address.
4. Return the security deposit.

Try to do these on the day (or day after) the tenant moves out if you can. Establish a convenient time with your departee to make a joint move-out inspection. That way, both you and your departing tenant can agree on what additional cleaning or repair work might need to be completed prior to his refund. Use the move-in/out inspection report for comparisons. Keep in mind that the outgoing tenant, after moving and cleaning all day, probably won't be in the best humor. Be thorough in your inspection, but also be as diplomatic as you can when you point out deficiencies.

If the outgoing tenant is unable or unwilling to complete the cleaning and/or repairs, let him know that you will determine costs, deduct them, and send him the balance of his deposit along with documentation of the deductions as soon as possible (and absolutely within the legally required time frame). Form # 23 in Appendix A is a good sample security deposit refund form. You could be fined by a court of law if you do not return the documented balance due within the required time.

You may need to pro-rate some of the repair costs between yourself and your departed tenant. For example, if the tenant has damaged a carpet that has only a year of its five-year life expectancy left, don't expect to get away with charging him with the total cost of a new carpet. Do document all deductions.

Also document your attempts to deliver the refund. If the refund is returned to you as undeliverable, keep it in the tenant's dead file for any legally required period of time.

Involuntary Terminations

Notice of Termination of Tenancy (form # 14)

Usually, if your tenant is on a month to month rental agreement, you can terminate the tenancy by serving him with a 30-Day Notice to Terminate the Tenancy. After legal service, the tenant has 30 days to move. You do not need to state the reason for the termination unless your rental is subject to certain rent control ordinances or is under some other form of government control. You may also need to give a valid reason if the tenant challenges the notice in court.

Notice to Pay Rent or Quit (form #16)

Different states have different time requirements for this notice: it could be a three-, five- or ten-day notice. The message is the same: pay the past due rent within the given time or leave. Most states limit the amount to be paid to the rent, although some may include other items such as late charges, utility bills, or damages. You may invalidate the notice if you accept a partial rent. In some jurisdictions you can note on your receipt that you are accepting the partial rent, but reserving the right to continue the eviction process. You may need to serve a new pay or quit notice after accepting a partial rent. Check with your lawyer for the procedure in your jurisdiction. If you handle this procedure incorrectly, you may have to start the whole process all over again, losing valuable time and money. It is very important to handle all these notices strictly by the book. Each state has different procedures on the steps to be taken if the tenant has not paid the past due rent after the time period is up. If you are unsure of the procedure in your state, I'd recommend that you have your attorney handle it. Procedural mistakes could be very expensive.

Three-Day Notice to Perform Conditions or Quit (form #17)

This notice, like a pay or quit notice, gives your tenant a choice. In this case the choice is: correct the breach of contract or leave. It can be used if the tenant violates a provision of the rental agreement, lease, house rules or regulations, or other condition of the rental. It can also be used if a tenant breaks the law or a local ordinance or involves the rental somehow in breaking the law. The break might involve police, fire, health or safety considerations.

In a month-to-month tenancy, you may choose to serve the tenant with a 30-day notice if the problem is serious or repeated. Common reasons for either type of notice include:

- provable unlawful activities

- unauthorized pets or extra people in violation of the rental contract
- trashing the property
- loud or obnoxious behavior

Avoiding this type of problem is the best reason for having well-written rental agreements and house rules, and for spending time with your applicant during the move-in orientation. If the tenant is doing something that you feel is unacceptable, but is not covered in your month-to-month agreements, you need to serve him a legal notice changing the terms of the tenancy. If he has a lease, you are stuck.

If the tenant fails to "cure" the breach within the legal time frame, you continue the eviction procedure.

Three-Day Notice to Quit for Breach of Convenant(s) (form #18)

This notice is similar to the "cure or quit" notice, but does not give the tenant a choice. It is used if the breach of contract is not "curable" or cannot be corrected.

Other Involuntary Causes for Terminations

Notice of Belief of Abandonment (form #20). An abandonment or suspected abandonment of a rental by a tenant is a frustrating experience for the owner. State laws differ in re-entry procedure, timing, notification, and other requirements. Tread carefully.

Death of Tenant. Even professional managers with large numbers of rentals rarely have to deal with this situation.

Call the authorities and your lawyer and do what they tell you to do.

Other situations may occur that terminate a tenancy involuntarily. Follow the procedure established by your state law and the advice of your attorney. These other situations include:

- hospitalization or incarceration of tenant
- foreclosure of the property
- destruction of the property
- sale of the property

Evictions

Constructive evictions

So called "constructive evictions " are illegal in most jurisdictions. They are the "self-help" tactics employed by unscrupulous landlords to evict tenants. They are demeaning and in some cases border on terrorism. They include locking the tenants out, throwing their personal possessions out in the street, shutting off necessary utilities, removing doors or toilets, or otherwise making the residence uninhabitable in an effort to evict a tenant. Even if your state has not gotten around to outlawing these questionable terror tactics, I recommend that you find other more humane and business-like methods of handling tenant problems.

Legal evictions

The legal process for handling evictions is determined by your state law. Follow it to the letter. The first step is the actual service of the eviction notice.

You or your agent may be required to serve the notice in person directly to the evictee(s) or you may be allowed to serve another person (substituted service) or you may be allowed to post the notice at the residence or you might be allowed to mail it. In any case, you will probably be required to provide "proof of service" (form #19) to the court.

The court itself might be a Small Claims Court, a Municipal Court, or a State Court. The amount you are claiming as "damages" usually has some bearing on the jurisdiction. Some jurisdictions may allow you to act "In Propria Persona," which means acting as your own attorney; some may not. Getting competent legal advice is always a good idea in an eviction. However you do it in your state, be prepared if you end up in court. Be sure to bring the following documentation:

- receipts for legitimate expenses
- appropriate ledgers
- the original rental agreement
- any additions or changes to the rental agreement
- photographs of damage
- any other documentation your attorney feels is appropriate

Even getting a court judgment may not allow you to collect money due you. Your battle for truth and justice must go on and depends on the law and the court system in your jurisdiction.

The following is a list of legal terms that you may not want to know, but that you may find useful if you are involved in an eviction proceeding.

- Breach of Contract: Breaking the terms or conditions of a lease

or rental agreement
- Complaint: A statement of the plaintiff's case
- Default: Failure to respond within an allotted period of time
- Defendant: The one against whom a case is brought; the party being sued
- Judgment: The outcome of the court trial
- Notice to Vacate: The Sheriff's or Marshall's final warning to the evictee to vacate the premises
- Plaintiff: The one bringing a case to court; the party suing
- Plaintiff in Pro Per: A Latin expression meaning the plaintiff is "in his own person" or representing himself
- Process Server: Someone who serves legal papers
- Request to Enter Default: A request for the court clerk to file the fact that the defendant failed to respond to the summons
- Service: Serving of legal papers
- Summons: A legal notice requiring one to appear in court
- Unlawful Detainer: Wrongly occupying property that belongs to someone else; the legal action necessary for eviction
- Writ of Execution: Written authority to the Sheriff or Marshall from the court to return possession of a designated property to its rightful owner

Tenant defenses

When faced with an eviction notice there are really only three actions a tenant can take. They are: move out, negotiate, or defend himself or herself in court.

What he decides to do often depends on his circumstances and whether he feels he may have a good defense.

If he chooses not to respond to the eviction notice, he might move out right away, or he might let you go through the whole process and wait until the last day to move.

If you have been communicating with your tenant all through the tenancy, you should be able to do so now that you are both facing a problem. If you cannot talk reasonably and logically with your renter at this point, then you are both in for a rough time, in terms of both stress and strain and financial cost. Evictions are usually unpleasant experiences for everyone involved.

The first reactions for both owner and tenant, especially when the rent is not paid, are often anger and resentment: not a good atmosphere for settling a problem.

If your tenant has been with you for a while, you are in a better position to gauge his sincerity and truthfulness (and he yours). You will have a better chance of reaching a satisfactory solution to the problem. Your discussions and negotiations with your tenant may even begin before the rent is due. He might call to let you know that for one reason or another he won't be able to meet the rent. If he has been a satisfactory tenant up to this point, do what you can to work it out. If he has not been a satisfactory tenant, do what you can to have him move out as soon as possible. Your negotiations with your tenant involve personal as well as legal considerations. Do seek legal help if necessary. The possibilities for negotiating are as endless as the situations that promote them.

Many of the rental owners I've talked to suggested paying your delinquent tenant a sum of money to help him move out. Judge for yourself if the circumstances justify that action as the quickest and least expensive way to solve the problem. Whatever solution you reach with your tenant, *put it in writing*. Put the particulars of your "negotiated settlement" in the form of a short contract.

If no settlement can be reached and for whatever reasons both you and your tenant decide to fight it out in court, the tenant has three basic methods to defend himself. They are actual defense, technical defense, or affirmative defense.

Depending on the situation, and his expertise, he may or may not use the services of an attorney. The same applies to you. Attorneys may not distinguish between these three types of defenses, and courts in your jurisdiction may not allow all of them. They are presented here only to make you aware of the possible defenses that may arise. Be prepared.

For purposes of this discussion, actual defenses are those that simply deny the accusations presented in your complaint. For example, you might state: Defendant failed to pay agreed-upon rent. The defendant's answer might be that he did offer to pay the rent and that the plaintiff (you) refused to accept it. In the case of a breach of contract eviction, you might state that contrary to your contract, the defendant kept a pet alligator in the bathroom. The defendant might answer that he got rid of the pet on such and such a date and is not in violation of the contract. Those are obviously simplified versions of potentially complex disputes.

The second type of defense could be called a technical defense and might include one or more of the following:

- eviction notice illegally served
- incorrect amount of overdue rent stated on the notice
- no notice served

These types of defense based on technicalities may be perfectly legal and may cause you to start the process all over again, successfully delaying the final eviction date.

Affirmative defenses bring up "facts" not addressed in your complaint and can often put you on the defensive. Examples are:

- The landlord breached his responsibility of providing a habitable residence by not complying with certain building code requirements.
- The eviction is illegal because it is based on the tenant's race.
- The eviction is an unlawful retaliation for the tenant's reporting violations to the rent control board.

There are more particulars on avoiding those types of situations in the chapters on Recordkeeping, Discrimination, Rights and Responsibilities, and Maintenance.

Some "affirmative defenses" are difficult to prove, but from your perspective they may be more difficult to disprove.

I know I've said it before, but it bears repeating: The best way to avoid the problems of an eviction is to do everything possible to get a qualified responsible renter in the first place.

This whole chapter on evictions has been, of necessity, very general. For specific advice for your situation, and in your jurisdiction, see your lawyer and get one of the excellent publications on the subject from your bookstore, library, or apartment association office.

CHAPTER 11

Everything You Always Wanted to Know About Maintenance

Maintenance is one of the keys to a successful rental business of any size. Properly maintaining your rentals makes sense from both an investment standpoint and a legal perspective. Well-maintained properties are worth more and usually get more rent. Poorly maintained rentals can cause more problems than they're worth. Habitability standards, as well as Health and Safety Codes vary considerably from state to state and city to city. Whatever they are in your jurisdiction, you, as a rental owner, need to be aware of them and make every effort to comply with them.

Types of Maintenance

There are two general categories of maintenance: routine and response. Routine maintenance chores can be scheduled. A good comprehensive maintenance schedule can prevent most of the response maintenance problems that seem always to occur when you have the least time for them. You need to run your properties, not let them run you. Don't wait until something goes wrong in the middle of the night before you fix it. Response maintenance could also be called crisis management.

The particulars of your maintenance plan or schedule depends on the structure itself and where it's located. For instance, if your rental is located where it snows heavily in winter, you'll have different considerations than owners with rentals in a desert area. Wherever your rental is, and whatever size, you'll need to schedule three basic types of routine maintenance:

1. Janitorial

2. Repair

3. Preventive Maintenance

Janitorial maintenance

Janitorial chores include the jobs itemized on the cleaning checklist shown in the sample form (#24). For those you'll need a standard assortment of brooms, mops, rags, and household cleaning solutions. For smaller rentals, you are usually only concerned with those jobs between tenants. Most renters in most situations can and do clean their own residence. The day-to-day interior cleaning of a rental is usually out of your hands.

Repairs

A good responsible tenant will advise you of needed repairs. Encourage them to do this. Typically, these are minor repair problems that can be handled quickly and easily, either by you or your renter. If your tenant is particularly inept at things mechanical, the problem might be solved over the phone by advising him to plug it in, push a reset button, replace a fuse, or turn on a switch.

The thought of repairs may not be a big deal for you. Some people are more mechanically inclined than others. There are many good references on home repairs in your library, bookstores, and building supply stores. Some claim that most people are capable of performing 80 to 90 percent of home repairs with 10 to 15 basic tools. If you do your own repair work, one or more of these "How To" books is essential.

You can save yourself a lot of money if you have a basic knowledge of electricity, plumbing, and carpentry. Most rental repairs involve such things as fixing plumbing leaks, replacing electrical outlets, unclogging plumbing, fixing toilets, replacing broken windows, and some occasional painting. Even for unhandy persons, they are typically only twos or threes on a ten-point difficulty scale. If you do need to call someone more qualified for a particular job, be sure to read Hiring a Contractor in this chapter.

The Maintenance Plan/Schedule

To set up a workable maintenance schedule for your rental, you'll need to:

1. Inspect the property

2. Determine your needs and priorities

3. Get information

4. Estimate time and materials needed

5. Decide who will do the work

Step one: inspect the property

When you inspect your rental look closely at the various components of both the buildings and the grounds. Normal wear and tear is a gradual process so be aware of it. Look for possible problems. You should make a thorough inspection of the following at least once or twice a year:

Exterior

- Roof: Check areas where leaks might start, such as flashing, chimneys, and so forth. Professional management companies and many owners rely on the services of a qualified roofing contractor to perform this inspection. Doing this one yourself could be dangerous for you and the building.
- Windows: Check for cracks in both the glass and the caulking.
- Siding: Whatever type of siding is on your rental, check it for cracks, splits, or weak areas that could allow moisture to get through.
- Eaves: Look for evidence of poor ventilation, dampness, and mildew.
- Balconies, stairs, and railings: As buildings age, they tend to settle and shift. Look for cracks, loose joints, and protruding nails.
- Gutters and downspouts: Check for split seams, pulled-apart joints, or clogged channels. Clean them out twice a year.
- Screens: For both window and door screens check for tears and loose molding.
- Paint: Check for peeling and splitting. Many owners and managers save painting expenses by painting the north and east sides of a building less frequently than the south and west sides, which get more sun exposure and tend to deteriorate faster.
- Paved surfaces, such as walkways, driveways, and patios: Check for cracks, holes, splits, or uneven settling.

Interior

- Plumbing: Look for leaks or moisture around joints, faucets, and toilets.

- Bathrooms: Check tubs and showers for loose, cracked, or broken caulking or grout. Repair immediately!
- Fans, pumps, and any other equipment with moving parts: Check for adequate lubrication. Oil as needed according to operating instructions.
- Filters: Change air conditioning and heating system filters at least twice a year, more often if necessary. They are very easy to do, easy to forget, and, if not changed periodically, can cause higher fuel bills by making the unit work harder. Keep a supply on hand.
- Electrical outlets and switches: Make sure they work and that the covers are not cracked or broken. Be especially aware of exposed wiring.

There are other things to check, but this list will get you started. Be thorough in your inspection. Keep copies of your inspection sheets and notes.

Step Two: Determine Your Needs and Priorities

Your inspection will point out areas that need attention. Determine which jobs need immediate attention and which can be deferred or scheduled later. Things that might affect the health and safety of your tenants need immediate attention. Schedule other tasks using the following priorities:

1. Habitability (wiring)
2. Cosmetic (paint)
3. Aesthetics (wallpaper)
4. Nuisance (squeaky garage door)

Step Three: Get Information

Once you've determined what needs to be done and when you plan to do it, you'll need some back-up information. Before you jump into any work you may need to have on hand:

- a complete set of up-to-date building plans, including plumbing and electrical diagrams
- equipment operating manuals
- valve location charts

- copy of local building code
- health and safety regulations
- instruction manuals for specific jobs, if necessary

All this material can be kept in your travel folder (see Chapter 2 on Recordkeeping).

Step Four: Estimate Time, Tools, and Materials Needed

After you know what needs to be done, you can figure out how long it might take and what equipment or materials are needed to get the job done. People at a good building supply store should be able to help you with this. Friends, neighbors, or people in the building trades might also be good sources of information if you're inexperienced.

Step Five: Determine Who Will Do the Work

Depending on your schedule, your skills, estimated costs, and the complexity of the job, you have several choices. The important thing to determine is which choice is the most cost-effective, the most economical way to get the job done. Here are some choices:

- Your tenant
- Yourself
- Handy persons
- Licensed professionals
- Contract service firms

Your tenant may be quite capable of performing some routine maintenance chores such as changing light bulbs, filters, light switch cover plates, and other simple procedures. If your tenant is ready, willing, and able to do this kind of task, make some sort of arrangement for him to take care of minor problems. The procedure should be outlined in your rental agreement or in an addendum.

You are the best judge of whether or not you are the appropriate person to do a particular job. If you are apprehensive about this aspect of your rental business, it might be best to work with a qualified friend to get the hang of repair procedures. If you expect several of the same types of job, you might just hire a pro the first time and observe how it's done.

A qualified, reliable "jack of all trades" is a vanishing breed. If you have someone like that who is trustworthy and available, treat that person right. If you are looking for a handy person, you might check with friends, neighbors, or other rental owners for references. You could also check the newspaper, Yellow Pages, or shopper newspapers.

Hiring A Contractor

If you do contract out some of the repair work, the Consumer's Resource Handbook, published by the United States Office of Consumer Affairs offers the following advice:

On home improvements

1. Get more than one estimate using the same specifications and materials.

2. Have a *written* contract that includes:
    *   the contractor's full name, address, phone number, and license number
    *   a thorough description of the work to be done
    *   the grade and quality of the materials to be used
    *   the agreed upon starting and completion dates
    *   the total cost, and payment schedule

3. Before you make your final payment, make a thorough inspection of the contractor's work.

4. If you sign the contract away from the seller's regular place of business, you will have a "three-day cooling off period." This means you have the right to cancel your contract anytime before midnight of the third business day after you sign the contract. Be sure a copy of the "Notice of Cancellation" form is included with your contract.

5. Inquire whether the contractor has liability and compensation insurance to protect you from lawsuits in the event of an accident.

6. If the work requires a building permit, let the contractor apply for it in his own name. If it is in your name and the work does not pass inspection, you will be responsible for any corrections that must be made.

7. Check with your county or city officials to see if the contractor is licensed and bonded. A bond will protect you against liens on the property if the contractor defaults with supplies and subcontractors. Also check with local consumer protection agencies. See Appendix B for a list of state consumer

protection agencies. Check with the Better Business Bureau to see if any complaints have been filed against the contractor.

On contracts

1. Never sign anything you do not understand.
2. Be sure that what the salesperson promises is what the contract says.
3. Don't sign a contract if a promoter or retailer is reluctant to let you have another person review it first.
4. Never sign a contract with unfilled spaces. Draw lines through blank spaces.

Areas where you will probably need professional help sooner or later include:

- electrical
- plumbing
- heating and air conditioning
- painting
- roofing
- major carpentry
- pest control

Tools and Supplies

No chapter on maintenance in a book about rental management would be complete without at least mentioning tools.

Peter Jones in his excellent home repair book, *Indoor Home Repairs Made Easy*, lists fifteen basic tools that he feels will take care of most home repairs. For rank beginners he recommends starting out with at least the following:

- sixteen-ounce claw hammer
- screwdrivers, including a Philips head and a standard blade
- folding rule or steel tape measure
- slip joint pliers and needle nose pliers
- wrenches, including an adjustable wrench, and a pipe wrench for plumbing repairs

Beyond those basics, he recommends that you add the following as needed:

- combination square, which he describes as "perhaps the most versatile of all measuring tools" as it can be used for measuring, marking, leveling, and plumbing
- clamps
- chisels
- block plane
- surform tool, which can be used for filing and planing wood, metal, plastics, and laminates
- taping knives
- electric power drill
- saber saw

I would add electrical tape, duct tape, a good sharp pocket knife, and assorted nails and screws to your supplies.

As a note to encourage beginners to begin, Mr. Jones says that professionals (electricians, plumbers, and carpenters) admit that many of the jobs they are called upon to do for homeowners could have been performed by the homeowner. He goes on to say that each profession has one rigid rule of the trade that must be unfailingly observed. They are:

- for electricians: Electricity must always travel in a complete circle.
- for plumbers: Every connection must be water tight.
- for carpenters: Every measurement must be precise.

Inventories

Keeping maintenance and repair supplies on hand is relative to the number of properties you have and how much of the work you do yourself. If you do keep maintenance inventories, keep in mind:

- emergency needs (fuses?)
- routine requirements (washers?)
- seasonal requirements (snow removal?)
- landscape maintenance supplies
- relative costs of keeping bulk items on hand (even though you got a great deal, do you really need a hundred gallons of paint, or a case of light bulbs?)

Entering The Unit

A word of caution before you enter a tenant's unit: Do everything possible to let the tenant know when you will be there. See Chapter 5 on tenant's rights for more specifics on why and how.

The first step for tenant-initiated repair requests is to have your renter use a form similar to #11 in Appendix A, the "Resident's Service Request." You can then follow up with a "Notice to Enter Dwelling Unit" (form #12). Even if your state does not require such a notice, it is always better to err on the side of caution.

CHAPTER 12

Attitudes and Aptitudes

Bud Gardner, a writer and writing instructor, gives a presentation at writing seminars entitled "Ten Steps To Becoming A Successful Writer." The more I reviewed my notes on those ten steps, the more I realized that they apply to most pursuits including life itself and managing your own rentals. With Bud's permission I am paraphrasing those steps to apply more specifically to the business of managing rentals. Most of us are aware of these principles to some degree but they are well worth reviewing to jog our consciousness occasionally.

Step One: Have a Winning Attitude

We all have limitations. Your attitude will enable you to go beyond your limitations, rather than use them as an excuse to stop or give up. Managing your own rentals is not always an easy task. The point is to concentrate on your goals and not be discouraged by those obstacles that keep popping up. The rental business can be enormously frustrating and discouraging, especially if you lose sight of your goals. Stick to it. Get beyond those obstacles and learn from your mistakes.

Having a positive attitude about your rental business is very important. Your attitude toward your tenant is critical. Every tenant is, after all, only human. Be fair; be reasonable; be legal; and don't be a chump! Don't overreact. The same judgments you apply to your tenant can be applied to you. Just because he's turned your beautiful rental into a half-way house for rodents and roaches is no reason to disregard the rules of the game. There are as many examples of bad landlords as there are of bad tenants. Ask any tenant.

Step Two: Get Serious About . . . Your Rental Business

Sometimes it is difficult to remember that your rentals are a business. You are providing a commodity for a fee. View your rentals with the same professionalism that you view your regular job, business, or profession. Establish lines of communication with your tenant (customer, client, account). *Be tenant oriented.* I know that it is your property. Just remember who is paying you to buy it.

Know as much as you can about your business. The landlord/tenant laws are constantly being rewritten and reinterpreted. Keep up to date with seminars, newsletters, articles. Keep notebooks and files. Read as much as you can. Join the local apartment owners' association. You might be surprised to know that most members of such organizations are like you; not the fat-cat landlord stereotypes that you might expect. These associations can be your prime source of information and forms vital to your rental business.

Step Three: Make An Unyielding Commitment

Take a stand that your rental business is productive and profitable. Regarding commitment, Goethe said it best:

> "Until one is committed, there is hesitancy, the chance to draw back, always ineffectiveness. Concerning all acts of initiative there is always one elementary truth the ignorance of which kills countless ideas and endless plans: that the moment one definitely commits oneself then providence moves too. All sorts of things occur to help one that would never otherwise have occurred. A whole stream of events issues from the decision, raising in one's favor all manner of unforeseen incidents and meetings and material assistance, which no man could have dreamed would come his way. Whatever you can do or dream you can, begin it! Boldness has genius, power, and magic in it."

Whew! Pretty heady stuff. Reread that quote whenever those hurdles and obstacles make you doubt your commitment.

Step Four: List Realistic Goals

Put your goals in writing. Why are you buying rentals? What do you intend for them to do for you in one month's time, in one year, five years, or ten years? How do you want your tenants to be? How do you want them to treat the property? How will owning and managing your own rentals enable you to reach your goals? Write it all down and review and reinforce it often.

Step Five: Have an Action Plan

I hate those trite old cliches as much as you do, but not enough not to use them. Here's one that makes sense: "Plan your work and work your plan." There are specific planning tools in the chapters on Recordkeeping and Maintenance. An action plan is similar to charting a course for a boat or airplane or car. You may know where you want to go, but without a specific plan it will take you longer to get there. Develop what the time management people call a time-line. Determine what needs to be done and when it is to be done. Then do it!

Step Six: Establish a Routine

Depending on the job to be done, you'll need to set aside time on a daily, weekly, or monthly basis.

If you have or expect to have a vacancy, you'll need to schedule time to show your unit properly. If you are not consistent in your scheduling you may lose an opportunity to establish a vital rapport with your prospective tenants.

Rent collecting, bill paying, and record keeping are functions for which routines should be established and followed religiously. Whatever your rent collection policy is, routinely enforce it. If you slack off, chances are your tenant will, too. Of all the routine chores we have in the rental business, the ones we least want to do are usually the ones we need to be most strict about.

For many routine tasks, it's simply a matter of fitting the job into your schedule. Others, however will demand that you alter your schedule to fit the task. In rentals, as in life, there are occasionally (some owners would opt for frequently here) unscheduled problems that need to be handled yesterday. Most often, though, establishing and sticking to routines will take a lot of the confusion and frustration out of your rental business.

Step Seven: Expect to Succeed

"Live your life, every day of it, with great expectations and great things will happen in your life daily." — *Art Fettig*

Did you ever start a project expecting to fail? What happened? Most likely you failed. The same principle applies to success. Expect to succeed and, chances are, you will.

That concept applies very directly in relating to your tenants. If you show your rental expecting the prospects to find fault and not rent it, your expectations will probably be fulfilled. Your expectations apply to all phases of the rental process. Ask yourself these questions.

- Do you expect to get good tenants?
- Do you expect the rent to be paid on time?
- Do you expect your tenants to respect your property?

Make your own list about what you expect from your rental. You'll probably get just what you expect to get. Doing your homework and properly preparing your rental will enable you to set realistic expectations. If you expect to get a $500 rent from a $200 dump, you're either stupid or living in a vacuum.

Expecting success does not necessarily mean you'll rent to the first qualified prospect that comes along. There may be temporary failures on your road to success. Persist.

Calvin Coolidge had this to say about persistence as it relates to success:

> "Nothing in the world can take the place of persistence.
> Talent will not; nothing is more common than unsuccessful men with talent.
> Genius will not; unrewarded genius is almost a proverb.
> Education will not; the world is full of educated derelicts.
> Persistence and determination alone are all-powerful."

Charles Garfield in his book *Peak Performance* says that top athletes actually visualize success. They see themselves performing and winning. Can you see yourself succeeding at the rental business? If not, get out. If you see the whole business defeating you, it will. Expect to succeed and you will!

Step Eight: Stop Procrastinating

In your rental business there are three areas where procrastination could be fatal:

1. Collecting the rent on time
2. Paying your bills on time
3. Responding to tenant requests on time

The first two are pretty obvious. The third is equally as important. Think of your tenants as paying customers and respond accordingly. Responding to tenant requests does not mean that you should jump every time your tenant snaps his fingers, but don't ignore him. Let him know what you're doing and when.

Dr. Wayne Dyer, in his best-selling self-awareness book *Your Erroneous Zones,* has some profound and illuminating things to say about procrastination. Here are just a few highlights:

> "Procrastination is really an escape from living present moments as fully as possible."

> "All wishing and hoping are a waste of time. No amount of either ever

got anything accomplished. They are merely convenient escape clauses from rolling up your sleeves and taking on the tasks that you've decided are important enough to be on your list of life activities."

Dr. Dyer goes on to compare critics and doers:

"It is easy to be a critic, but being a doer requires effort, risk and change."

If you expect to own and operate your own rentals efficiently and effectively, you must be a doer. If you are not, hire someone who is. Avoiding confrontations with others is one example of typical procrastinating behavior. If you have rentals, you can expect occasional confrontations. Often wishing to avoid confrontations is simply another way of wishing to avoid confronting our fear of failure and rejection. If we avoid the confrontation in the first place maybe we can avoid the failure or rejection. Not so, unfortunately.

Step Nine: Confronting the Fear of Failure and Rejection

When I think of failure and rejection as they relate to the business of rentals, rent collecting and evictions immediately come to mind. In performing both jobs, I've faced failure and rejection, sometimes violently. I have been yelled at, threatened, had my ancestry questioned, doors slammed in my face, and a few other unpleasantries not worth mentioning here. Fear of failing and fear of being rejected, however, are distinct from failure and rejection. Since these are psychological matters, I'll again refer to the words of wisdom offered by Dr. Dyer:

On Fear:

"Most of the reasons you'd give yourself for not operating from strength involve some kind of fear of 'what will happen if...'"

"Fear is internal and is supported by a neat little system of thoughts which you use to avoid dealing with your self-imposed dread. These thoughts may be expressed as:
I'll fail.
I'll look stupid.
They might not like me.
They might get mad at me"

"Doing is the antidote to fear. You cannot learn anything, undermine any fear, unless you are willing to DO something."

On Failure

"Failure does not exist."

"Failure is simply someone else's opinion of how a certain act should have been completed."

"Animals don't fail. They either do or do not. Natural behavior simply is."

"Why not apply the same logic to your own behavior and rid yourself of the fear of failure."

You may be rejected in some of your efforts. So what! Don't quit. Accept rejection and move on.

Step Ten: Think Like a Professional

This is really just a recap of Step Two. Have the discipline to learn as much as you can about the business that you are in. Stay informed. Treat your tenants fairly and with the respect they deserve as members of the human race.

APPENDIX A

Sample Forms

1. Application to Rent
2. Month-to-Month Rental Agreement
3. Long-Form Lease
4. Addendum to Rental Agreement and/or Lease
5. Rules & Regulations: House Rules
6. Furniture Inventory
7. Waterbed and/or Liquid-Filled Furniture Agreement
8. Pet Agreement
9. Conditions of Premises
10. Check In/Out Report
11. Resident's Service Request
12. Notice to Enter Dwelling Unit
13. Notice of Change of Terms of Tenancy
14. Notice of Termination of Tenancy
15. Thirty-Day Notice of Resident's Intent to Vacate
16. Notice to Pay Rent or Quit
17. Three-Day Notice to Perform Conditions or Quit
18. Three-Day Notice to Quit for Breach of Covenant(s)
19. Declaration of Service of Notice to Resident (Tenant)
20. Notice of Belief of Abandonment
21. Notice of Right to Reclaim Abandoned Personal Property (Value less than $300.00)
22. Notice of Right to Reclaim Abandoned Personal Property (Value more than $300.00)
23. Itemized Disposition of Security Deposit

24. Cleaning Checklist
25. Tenant Ledger (payment record)
26. Repair Record (work order)
27. Petty-Cash Voucher Envelope
28. Cash Receipt

Note: The following forms are a composite of rental forms from a variety of sources. They have been edited, altered, and paraphrased. No representation is made as to their authenticity or legality. They are presented strictly as possible examples of available rental forms. The author strongly urges the reader to obtain current and up-to-date rental forms from reliable sources such as apartment or rental associations, real estate boards, or consumer affairs offices.

#1: Application to Rent (a)

Each adult occupant must complete individual application

Last Name	First Name	Middle Name	SS#

Date of Birth	Drivers Lic. #, State	Home Phone #

Current Address

Date moved in	Date moved out	Owner/Mgr Name, Ph. #

Reason for moving

Previous Address

Date moved in	Date moved out	Owner/Mgr Name, Ph. #

Reason for Moving

List all additional proposed occupants names and ages

Current Occupation	Employer
How long?	Address
Supervisor	Phone #

Current Gross Income (per week, mo, or yr) attach verification

List ALL financial obligations

Bank	Address
Account #'s	Checking and Savings

Name of Creditor	Address
Phone	Payment

#1: Application to Rent (b)

Personal References	Address	Phone	Occupation
1.			
2.			
3.			

Emergency Information:

Notify: Name	Address	Phone	Relationship
1.			
2.			

Automobile: Make	Model	Year	License #
1.			
2.			

Other Vehicles (motorcycle, RV, Boat) to be at rental

Have you ever been evicted?

Have you ever filed for bankruptcy?

The undersigned makes application to rent housing:(description, location)for which the agreed upon rent is $_____ per_____ and upon approval of this application agrees to sign a rental agreement and pay all sums due prior to occupancy.

The undersigned states that all above information is true and accurate and hereby authorizes verification of the above information and agrees to furnish additional information or verification as needed.

_____   _____
                Applicant   Date

#1: Application to Rent (c)

Purpose of Application

1. The purpose of this application is to qualify applicants
2. It provides information about credit and rental history
3. It discourages unqualified applicants
4. It helps to trace "skips", and helps collections
5. It provides market information
6. It helps protect rental owners and managers from discrimination complaints
7. It saves the owner/mgr time, effort, and money
8. The prospective tenant needs to convince the owner/mgr:

    A) He/she can and will pay the rent on time

    B) She/he will not disturb neighbors or other tenants

    C) He/she will take care of the property

Rental Policy

1. Establish fair, consistent and uniform rental policies
2. Treat all applicants equally. Do not illegally discriminate
3. Know local rental ordinances

Preliminary Screening

1. To save everyone time and effort, determine prior to completion of application:

    A) When applicant wants to move in. Will unit be ready?

    B) Will applicant have required move in money?

    C) Does applicant have a pet or is otherwise disqualified?

2. Keep notes of this "interview"

Preparing The Rental Application

1. Each adult who is going to occupy the unit must complete and sign a separate application.
2. The application should be filled out in owner/manager's presence to eliminate incompleteness and misunderstandings.
3. Verbally review written information.
4. Advise applicant of pertinent rental policies (ie:no waterbeds).
5. Ask for two forms of identification.

#1: Application to Rent (d)

Verifying Application Information

1. Check information as soon as possible.
2. Advise applicant as soon as possible.

What to check on the application

1. Verify EVERYTHING!
2. Contact current landlord to determine timely payment of rent and treatment of unit.
3. Contact previous landlord, whose information may be more reliable than current landlord.
4. When checking employment get reliable unbiased information from company Personnel Department, not from immediate supervisor. Verify that company name, location, and phone number are authentic.
5. Verify checking account by calling applicants listed bank, giving account number and asking if check for rental amount will clear.
6. If at all possible run a credit check on applicant through local apartment association.

RED FLAGS!

1. DO NOT discard any application, even if you turn down applicant. Note why applicant was turned down and when. If applicant complains of discrimination, these notes should help.
2. Be absolutely positive that the person who authorized you to verify the rental application information is the correct person.
3. Update the form as needed.

#2: Month-to-Month Rental Agreement (a)

This Agreement, by and between

_____ and _____
(Owner/Landlord)   (Resident/Tenant)

entered into _____, in consideration of their mutual promises agree as follows:
(date)

1. Owner rents to Resident and Resident rents from Owner, for residential use only, the

premises known as: _____.
(address including state and zip code)

2. Rent is due in advance on the _____ day of each and every month, in the amount of

$_____ per month, beginning on _____.
(day/date)

3. Except as provided by law, this agreement may be terminated by either party after

legal service upon the other of a written 30 day Notice of Termination of Tenancy.

4. Premises shall be occupied by the following named person(s) only:

_____   _____

_____   _____

5. No animal, waterbed, or_____ shall be kept or allowed

in or about premises.

6. Resident shall not violate any Governmental law in the use of the premises.

7. No repairs, decorations, or alterations shall be done by Resident, without Owner's written

consent, except as provided by law.

8. Resident has inspected the premises, furnishings, equipment,including plumbing, heating

and electrical systems and found them to be satisfactory.

9. Resident shall keep the premises and any furniture, furnishings, and appliances in good

order and condition. Resident shall pay Owner costs to repair any portion of the premises

damaged by Resident or his guests. Resident's personal property is not insured by Owner.

#2: Month-to-Month Rental Agreement (b)

10. Resident shall pay for all utilities, services and charges, predicated upon occupancy of the unit, except: _____.

11. The undersigned Resident(s) are jointly and severally liable for all obligations under this rental agreement.

12. Resident shall deposit with Owner the sum of $_____ as a security deposit. Owner may withhold from this deposit only reasonable and necessary amounts to remedy tenant defaults as follows:

  A) payment of rent, or   B) to repair tenant caused damage to the premises,or

  C) to clean premises, if necessary, upon being vacated.

13. In the event of any legal action brought by either party to enforce the terms of this agreement, the prevailing party shall recover, in addition to all other relief, reasonable attorney's fees and costs.

14. Notice upon Owner may be served upon:_____ at:_____.

15. No portion of premises shall be sublet. Any attempted subletting shall be considered breach of this agreement.

16. Attachments: By initialling below, resident acknowledges receipt of indicated attachments.

A) House Rules_____

B) Pet Agreement_____

C) Inventory_____

D) Addendum_____

The undersigned resident has read and understood the foregoing and has received a duplicate original.

_____   _____
      Owner   Resident

#3: Long-Form Lease (a)

This Agreement, by and between _____ and _____
                                        (Owner/Landlord)   (Resident/Tenant)

entered into_____, in consideration of their mutual promises agree as follows:
            (Date)

1. Owner rents to Resident and Resident rents from Owner, for residential use only, the

premises known as: _____.
                                    (address including state and zip code)

2. Rent is due in advance on the _____ day of each and every month, in the amount of

$_____ per month, beginning on_____.
                            (day/date)

3. The term of this agreement is for _____ beginning on_____

and ending on_____, at which time the lease shall terminate without further

notice. A "month to month" tenancy shall be created only if Owner accepts rent from

Resident thereafter.

4. Premises shall be occupied by the following named person(s) only:

_____   _____

_____   _____

5. No animal, waterbed, or_____ shall be kept or allowed in or about premises.

6. Resident shall not violate any Governmental law in the use of the premises.

7. No repairs, decorations, or alterations shall be done by Resident, without Owner's written

consent, except as provided by law.

8. Resident has inspected the premises, furnishings, equipment,including plumbing, heating

and electrical systems and found them to be satisfactory.

9. Resident shall keep the premises and any furniture, furnishings, and appliances in good

order and condition. Resident shall pay Owner costs to repair any portion of the premises

damaged by Resident or his guests. Resident's personal property is not insured by Owner.

#3: Long-Form Lease (b)

10. Resident shall pay for all utilities, services and charges, predicated upon occupancy of the unit, except: _____.

11. The undersigned Resident(s) are jointly and severally liable for all obligations under this rental agreement.

12. Resident shall deposit with Owner the sum of $_____ as a security deposit. Owner may withold from this deposit only reasonable and necessary amounts to remedy tenant defaults as follows:

 A) payment of rent, or

 B) to repair tenant caused damage to the premises, or

 C) to clean premises, if necessary, upon being vacated.

13. In the event of any legal action brought by either party to enforce the terms of this agreement, the prevailing party shall recover, in addition to all other relief, reasonable attorney's fees and costs.

14. Notice upon Owner may be served upon:_____ at:_____.

15. No portion of premises shall be sublet. Any attempted subletting shall be considered breach of this agreement.

16. Waiver Provision

17. The Resident shall not keep upon said premises any item or permit any acts which will cause an increase in the insurance rate or endanger premises.

18. The Owner, his employees, or agents may enter the premises:

 A) In case of emergency, or

 B) When resident has surrendered or abandoned the premises, or

 C) To make necessary repairs or improvements, or to supply necessary or agreed services, or to show the unit to prospective purchasers, tenants, lenders, or workmen, provided the Resident is given reasonable notice of Owner's intent to enter.

#3: Long-Form Lease (c)

19. In the event that Resident breaches this agreement, Owner shall be allowed to exercise any or all remedies provided by State Civil Code Section XXXX.

20. Attachments: By initialling below, resident acknowledges receipt of indicated attachments.

A) House Rules   _____

B) Pet Agreement   _____

C) Inventory   _____

D) Addendum   _____

The undersigned resident has read and understood the foregoing and has received a duplicate original.

_____   _____
              Owner   Resident

#3: Long-Form Lease (d)

1. The purpose of the Long Form Lease is to state clearly the agreed upon terms by both the Owner and the Resident. It becomes a legally binding and enforceable contract when completed and signed by both parties.

2. Always use an up-to-date written rental agreement.

3. Prepare the forms and have them signed by all parties before you give the tenant the keys.

4. Use a Long Form Lease when you are leasing the unit for a specified period of time, usually, but not necessarily, one year.

5. Use a Month-to-Month agreement in all other situations.

6. Always show the date the agreement was signed and the full and complete names of all adult occupants.

7. Show complete physical address of the rental property.

8. Include rental amounts and dates.

9. The Owner, or his agent, must sign the lease agreement, as well as ALL adult occupants of the unit.

10. Always keep the signed original as your file copy.

11. Provide carbon copies to all other parties signing the agreement.

12. RED FLAG! The Long Form Lease becomes a Month-to-Month rental agreement if you accept rent from the tenant after the lease termination date.

#4: Addendum to Rental Agreement and/or Lease

This agreement is entered into _____, by and
                              (Date)
between_____, and
                  (Owner/Landlord)

_____ in consideration of mutual promises, Owner
        (Resident/Tenant)

and Resident agree as follows:

1. Resident is renting from Owner the premises located at:

_____.
                    (Complete Address)

2. This agreement is an Addendum and part of the Lease or Rental Agreement between

Owner and Resident.

_____

_____

_____

_____

_____

3. This Addendum is effective as of _____
                                         (Date)

_____   _____
        Owner   Resident

#5: Rules & Regulations: House Rules (a)

1. These house rules are part of the rental agreement dated
   _____.

2. Resident is responsible for the conduct of his guests.

3. Residents shall not make or allow disturbing noises in the unit.

4. All musical instruments and other noise producing devices are to be played at a volume which will not disturb other persons.

5. The activities and conduct of the resident, his children, his guests, their children, in or around the rental unit must be reasonable and responsible at all times.

6. No lounging, visiting or boistrous obstreprousness that may be disturbing to other residents will be allowed in any common areas between the hours of _____ and _____.

7. The unit must be kept clean and sanitary.

8. No littering is allowed.

9. No trash or hazardous material in violation of any health or safety code anywhere, anytime is permitted.

10. Garbage is to be placed inside the appropriate container only.

11. Inside furniture must be kept inside the unit.

12. No personal property is to be left in hallways or other common areas.

13. Clothing, curtains, rugs, and so forth shall not be shaken or hung from windows, ledges,or balconies.

14. All doors must be kept locked when resident is absent from the unit.

15. All appliances must be turned off before resident leaves the unit.

16. Smoking in bed is prohibited.

17. The use and/or storage of gasoline, solvents and other combustibles in the unit is prohibited.

18. The use of charcoal is prohibited in or out of the unit unless permission is obtained from the owner.

#5: Rules & Regulations: House Rules (b)

19. Children on the premises must be supervised by a responsible adult at all times.

20. The resident is responsible for checking the operating condition of all smoke detectors in the unit and for advising the owner in writing of any defect or malfunction of same.

21. Resident shall advise owner, in writing, of any needed repairs. Repair requests should be made when the problem is noted.

22. Costs of repair for any damage caused by the tenant are the responsibility of the tenant and must be paid on demand.

#6: Furniture Inventory

On _____, the undersigned resident carefully inspected the
            (Date)

furniture and furnishings located in the rental unit at_____and

found each item to be:

    A) Undamaged and in good working order;

    B) Adequate and appropriate for customary use;

    C) Free of vermin and in clean, sanitary condition,

unless noted and explained below.

Item Name	Location	Condition

Comments:_____

_____

_____

Resident acknowledges receipt of copy:

_____   _____
            Resident   Owner

#7: Waterbed and/or Liquid-Filled Furniture Agreement (a)

This agreement entered into this date_____, by and between

_____,Owner/Landlord, and_____,

Resident/Tenant, in consideration of their mutual promises agree as follows:

1. Resident is renting from owner the rental unit located at

_____.

2. The Rental Agreement provides that without owner's prior written consent, no waterbed

or other liquid filled furniture shall be allowed in or about said premises.

3. Resident wishes to keep the below listed "items", in or about the rental unit:

_____

_____

4. This agreement is a part of the rental agreement between owner and resident. In the

event of default by resident of any of the terms, resident agrees to cure the default or

vacate the premises. Owner may revoke permission to kepp "items" on the premises by

giving resident 30 day written notice.

5. As additional security, resident agrees to pay owner the sum of $_____. Owner

may deduct reasonable amounts from this deposit necessary to repair any damage

caused by "item".

6. Resident agrees to provide owner with a valid certificate of Waterbed Liability Insurance

with a minimum policy limit of $100,000.00 for property damage and bodily injury. Owner

is to be notified by the insurance company of any change or cancellation of said policy.

7. Resident agrees to comply with:

A) appropriate Building Code Requirements;

B) Health and Safety Codes;

C) any other applicable governmental regulations.

#7: Waterbed and/or Liquid-Filled Furniture Agreement (b)

8. Resident agrees to use a mattress, a safety liner, and a frame. If a heater is provided by the resident and the owner pays for the utilities for the heater, resident will pay the owner a sum of $_____per month for added utility costs.

9. Resident agrees to have qualified personel install "items" according to the manufacturers' specifications. Cost of installation is the responsibility of the resident.

10. Resident shall be liable to owner for all damages or expenses incurred by "item", and shall hold owner harmless for any and all damages.

11. To prevent injury or damage in an emergency, resident agrees to remove item immediately. If resident fails to do so , owner may remove item.

_____   _____
        Owner   Resident

#8: Pet Agreement

This agreement entered into this date_____, by and

between_____,Owner/Landlord, and _____,

Resident/Tenant, in consideration of their mutual promises agree as follows:

1. Resident is renting from owner the rental unit located at

_____.

2. The Rental Agreement provides that without owner's prior written consent, no pets shall be allowed in or about said premises.

3. Resident wishes to keep the below described pet in or about the rental unit:

_____

4. This agreement is a part of the rental agreement between owner and resident. In the event of default by resident of any of the terms, resident agrees to cure the default or vacate the premises. Owner may revoke permission to keep Pet on the premises by giving resident 30 day written notice.

5. As additional security, resident agrees to pay owner the sum of $_____. Owner may deduct reasonable amounts from this deposit necessary to repair any damage caused by Pet.

6. Resident agrees to comply with:
   A) Health and Safety Code, and
   B) any other applicable governmental regulations.

7. Resident represents that Pet(s) is (are) quiet and "housebroken" and will not cause any damage or annoy any other resident.

8. Resident agrees that Pet will not be permitted outside the resident's unit, unless restrained by a leash.

9. If Pet is a cat:
   A) It must be neutered and declawed, and
   B) resident must provide and maintain an appropriate litter box.

10 If Pet is a bird, it shall not be let out of the cage.

11. If fish, the water container shall not be over_____lbs., and must be placed in a safe location in the unit.

12. No Pet shall be fed on unprotected carpet within the unit. Resident shall prevent any fleas or other infestation of the rental unit or property of the owner.

#9: Conditions of Premises (a)

On_____, the undersigned carefully inspected the rental unit
        (date)
located at_____ and unless checked and explained
below, each item has been found:
    A) to be undamaged and in good working order;
    B) adequate and appropriate for customary use;
    C) free of vermin and in clean, sanitary condition.

Appliances

___ Air Conditioning   ___ Oven   ___ Stove
___ Dishwasher   ___ Range fan   ___ _____
___ Garbage Disposal   ___ Refrigerator   ___ _____

Coverings

___ Blinds   ___ Linoleum   ___ Sun Glare   ___ _____
___ Carpeting   ___ Rods   ___ Floor Tile   ___ _____
___ Drapes   ___ Shades   ___ Vinyl   ___ _____

Electrical

___ Covers   ___ Lighting   ___ Outlets   ___ _____
___ Doorbell   ___ Light bulbs   ___ Switches   ___ _____
___ Exhaust fan   ___ Fixtures   ___ Thermostat   ___ _____

Miscellaneous

___ Cabinets   ___ Keys   ___ Medicine Cabinet
___ Counters   ___ Locks   ___ Towel Bars
___ Drawers   ___ Mailbox   ___ _____

Outside Areas

___ Carport   ___ Lawns   ___ Trees
___ Garage   ___ Parking   ___ Stairs
___ Grounds   ___ Patio   ___ _____
___ Pool/Spa   ___ _____   ___ _____

Plumbing

___ Bathtub/Shower   ___ Heating   ___ Toilet
___ Cold water   ___ Hot water   ___ Sinks
___ Faucets   ___ Laundry   ___ _____

#9: Conditions of Premises (b)

Structure

___ Baseboards	___ Door jambs	___ Steps
___ Ceilings	___ Floors	___ Walls
___ Doors	___ Roof	___ Windows
___ _____	___ _____	___ _____

Comments:

_____

_____

_____

_____

Description of any defects noted:

_____

_____

_____

_____

Resident has received copy of this report:

_____   _____
              Resident   Owner

#10: Check In/Out Report

	In	CONDITION	Out
Kitchen			
Walls			
Floor			
Ceiling			
Range			
Exhaust fan			
Refrigerator			
Sink			
Cupboard			
Disposal			
Outlets			
Other			
Bathroom			
Tub			
Shower			
Sink			
Toilet			
Closet			
Cupboards			
Faucets			
Towel Rack			
Walls			
Ceiling			
Floor			
Other			
Living Room			
Carpet			
Walls			
Ceiling			
Doors			
Windows			
Drapes			
Outlets			
Other			
Bedrooms			
Doors			
Closets			
Carpet			
Windows			
Walls			
Ceiling			
Outlets			
Drapes			
Other			

Resident	Owner
Date	Date

#11: Resident's Service Request

1. Resident(s) Name _____
   Rental Address/ Unit _____
   Telephone (home) _____ (work) _____
   Time _____ Date _____

2. Service Requested:
   _____
   _____
   _____
   _____

3. Authorization: Owner/ Manager/Service person(s) are authorized to enter unit if
   Resident(s) is (are) not home unless otherwise instructed.

   _____, if verbal, by _____
            Resident's Signature

4. Instructions to Service Personnel:
   _____
   _____
   _____
   _____
   _____

5. Action Taken:
   Describe nature of problem, work done and materials used:
   _____
   _____
   _____
   _____
   _____

   Time spent completing service request: _____
   Date Completed: _____

6. Charge costs as follows:
   _____
   _____
   _____
   _____

7. Resident certifies that report is accurate: _____
   Exceptions: _____

   Date _____ Resident's Signature _____

#12: Notice to Enter Dwelling Unit

Pursuant to State Civil Code Section XYZ, Owner does hereby give notice to:

_____, and all persons in occupancy of the

premises located at: _____,

that owner, owner's agent or owner's employees will enter said premises on or

about_____ for the reason noted below:
               Day and Time

1. To make necessary or agreed repairs

2. Alterations or improvements

3. Decorations

4. Supply services

5. Exhibit the dwelling to prospective purchasers

6. Exhibit the dwelling to lenders

7. Exhibit the dwelling to prospective tenants

8. Exhibit the dwelling to contractors or workmen

9. Per Court Order

Date: _____   _____
                                         Owner/ Agent

#13: Notice of Change of Terms of Tenancy (a)

To:_____and to all others in possession

of the premises known as: _____
                                                  Complete unit address

You are hereby notified, in accordance with State Civil Code Section ABC that 30 days

after service upon you of this notice, or_____, whichever is later, your
                                              Date

tenancy of the above designated premises will be changed as follows:

1. The monthly rent which is payable in advance on or before the _____day of each

month will be the sum of $_____ instead of $_____, the current monthly rent.

2. Other Changes: _____
_____
_____
_____
_____

Except as herein provided, all other terms of your tenancy shall remain.

Date: _____   _____
                                                  Owner/Agent

#13: Notice of Change of Terms of Tenancy (b)

1. The purpose of this form is to provide the essential legal terminology when you wish to change the terms or increase the rent on a month to month rental agreement.

2. It is always good for tenant relations to send a cover letter explaining the notice.

3. List the full names of all adults named in the rental agreement as well as any other adult residents.

4. Give the complete rental address.

5. Remember that the effective date of the change needs to be more than 30 days from the date of service.

6. Be specific when describing the changes.

7. Be sure to sign the notice and date it accurately.

8. Keep the original copy.

9. Serve a copy to each and every adult resident.

10. The notice must be served in the legally proscribed manner.

11. Red Flags: In Section 8 and rent control housing, specific guidelines must be strictly followed.

#14: Notice of Termination of Tenancy (a)

To:_____
(full names of ALL adult tenants in possession)

Please take notice that your tenancy of the below described premises is terminated,

effective at the end of a thirty (30) day period after service on you of this notice,
or_____,

(Date)

whichever is later.

Premises:_____

_____
(complete rental address)

Date: _____
Owner/ Agent

#14: Notice of Termination of Tenancy (b)

1. The purpose of this form is to provide the owner with the proper legal form to regain possession of rental property.

2. The resident is allowed 30 days, after proper service, to vacate the property, if he is on a month to month rental term and local rent control ordinances do not prohibit it.

3. If the tenant is on a lease, this form can be used 30 days before lease expiration to terminate the lease.

4. It is important to include the names of all adult tenants exactly as they appear on the rental agreement or lease.

5. Be sure to fill out the complete address, and date , and sign the notice.

6. Keep the original copy for court use, one copy for yourself, and two copies for each person named on the notice.

7. At the end of the 30 day period, if the resident has not vacated, an Unlawful Detainer action needs to be initiated.

8. NO Reason need be given for the notice. Giving a reason may complicate the Unlawful Detainer action.

9. Seriously consider helping the tenant to relocate. Court battles are expensive and time consuming.

10. If the tenant has filed a complaint prior to the notice, the notice may be considered as a retaliatory eviction and could cause lengthy delays in the process.

11. Specific rules must be followed in Rent Control and Section 8 housing situations.

#15: Thirty-Day Notice of Resident's Intent to Vacate

To: (Owner/Agent) _____

You are hereby given notice that the undersigned intends to terminate the tenancy and to

move from the premises known as: _____,

as of _____.
          (Date)

It is understood as follows:

   A) that this notice is required by State Civil Code Section 123.4 and
   B) except as provided by law, rent shall be due and payable to and including the
      date of termination or thirty (30) days after service of this notice on the owner,
      whichever is later.

After all the undersigned's possessions are removed from the premises, the undersigned
will notify the owner/agent and return the keys.

The undersigned's reason for terminating the rental agreement is as follows:

_____

_____

_____

Forwarding Address: _____

                           _____

                           _____

Date: _____   _____
                                        Resident

#16: Notice to Pay Rent or Quit (a)

To: _____

                    (full names of ALL adult tenants in possession)

Within three days after the service on you of this notice, you are required to pay to the

undersigned or his authorized agent,_____, the rent of the

premises hereinafter described, of which you now hold possession amounting to the sum

of_____ enumerated as follows:

$_____Due from_____to_____or quit and

deliver up the possession of the premises.

The premises herein referred to are:

_____

You are further notified that, the owner/landlord does hereby elect to declare the

forfeiture of your lease or rental agreement under which you hold possession of the

above described premises and if you fail to comply, will institute legal proceedings to

recover rent and possession of said premises.

Date: _____   _____

                                      Owner/Agent

#16: Notice to Pay Rent or Quit (b)

1. Once the rent is past due, a Notice to Pay Rent or Quit should be served on the resident.

2. It is absolutely essential that this notice be filled out correctly. If you need to go to court to seek an eviction, an improperly filled out form will cause the case to be dismissed.

3. Be certain that the names of the evictees, the amount due, and the address of the residence are correct. If incorrect you will not be able to evict until you serve a correct notice.

4. Consult an attorney if you have any doubts or apprehensions.

#17: Three-Day Notice to Perform Conditions or Quit

To:_____

(full names of ALL adult tenants in possession)

Please take notice that you are in violation of the terms of your rental agreement of the

premises located at: _____

in that, the rental agreement/lease conditions set forth below are being breached as

follows:

1. Conditions breached:

_____

_____

_____

_____

2. Specific facts of breach or violations:

_____

_____

_____

_____

Within three days after the service on you of this notice, you are hereby required to

perform or otherwise comply with the above mentioned condition or quit and deliver up

the possession of the premises.

You are further notified that, the owner/landlord does hereby elect to declare the

forfeiture of your lease or rental agreement under which you hold possession of the

above described premises and if you fail to comply, will institute legal proceedings to

recover rent and possession of said premises.

Date: _____   _____

                                     Owner/Agent

18: Three-Day Notice to Quit for Breach of Covenant(s)

To:_____

(full names of ALL adult tenants in possession)

Please take notice that you are in violation of the terms of your rental agreement of the

premises located at: _____

in that, the rental agreement/lease condition(s) and/or covenants set forth below are

being breached as follows:

1. Condition(s) and/or Covenants breached:

_____
_____
_____
_____

2. Specific facts of breach or violations:

_____
_____
_____
_____

    Within three days after the service on you of this notice, you are hereby required to quit

and deliver up the possession of the premises.

    You are further notified that, the owner/landlord does hereby elect to declare the

forfeiture of your lease or rental agreement under which you hold possession of the

above described premises and if you fail to comply, will institute legal proceedings to

recover possession of said premises.

Date: _____   _____
                                                 Owner/Agent

#19: Declaration of Service of Notice to Resident (Tenant) (a)

I, the undersigned, declare that at the time of service of the papers herein referred to, I

was at least eighteen (18) years of age , and that I served the following notice:

___ Notice to Pay Rent or Quit

___ Thirty (30) Day Notice of Termination of Tenacy

___ Other_____

on the following resident(s)

_____

on _____
                 Date

___ By Delivering a copy of the Notice to each of the above named resident(s) personally.

OR

___ By Leaving a copy for each of the above named resident(s) with a person of suitable
age and discretion at the residence or usual place of business of the resident(s), said
resident being absent thereof;

And Mailing by first class mail on said date a copy to each resident by depositing said
copies in the United States Mail, in a sealed envelope, with postage fully prepaid,
addressed to the above named resident(s) at their place of residence.

OR

___ By Posting a copy for each of the above named resident(s) in a conspicuous place
on the property therein described there being no person of suitable age or discretion to
be found at any known place of residence or business of said resident(s);

And Mailing by first class mail on said date a copy to each resident by depositing said
copies in the United States Mail, in a sealed envelope, with postage fully prepaid,
addressed to the above named resident(s) at their place of residence.

I declare under penalty of perjury that the foregoing is true and correct and if called as a
witness to testify thereto, I could do so competently.

Executed _____ at _____.
                    Date   Location

_____
                        Signature of Declarant

#19: Declaration of Service of Notice to Resident (Tenant) (b)

1. The "Declaration of Service" form must be filled out by the person who actually serves the notice.

2. A person must be 18 years of age or older to legally serve a notice.

3. An owner or manager may serve any notices. An owner may NOT serve the Summons and Complaint in an Unlawful Detainer action.

4. The name of the person(s) on the Rental Agreement, the Notice, and the Declaration must be correct.

5. Serve each party individually.

6. The Declaration indicates three types of service:

   Personal: Service must be made in person, unless the person cannot be found at the residence or their usual place of business.

   Substituted: A copy of the notice must be left with a responsible person of suitable age and discretion at the residence or place of business, and a copy mailed, prepaid first class, to the residence.

   Constructive: The notice may be affixed on the property, and a copy mailed (prepaid, first class), if a responsible person cannot be found.

7. The notice must be dated and signed correctly.

8. Submit the completed, original form to the court at the time of the hearing. Keep a copy in your file.

9. Use a separate Declaration of Service for each party, if you serve different parties different ways.

10. The day of service does not count as a day. Start your count the next day.

#20: Notice of Belief of Abandonment (a)

To:_____
                    Full Name of ALL Adult Residents

The premises herein referred to as _____

This notice is given concerning the property rented by you at the above described

address. The rent on the property has been due and unpaid for 14 or more consecutive

days and the landlord believes that you have abandoned the property.

The property will be deemed abandoned and your tenancy shall terminate on

_____, which is not less than 18 days after this notice is deposited in

the mail unless before that date the undersigned receives a written notice from you

stating:

1.   Your intent not to abandon the real property.

2.   An address at which you may be served by certified mail in any action for
      unlawful detainer of the real property.

You are required to pay the rent due and unpaid on this property as required by the rental

agreement and your failure to do so could lead to a court proceeding against you.

Date of mailing of this notice _____

_____
Owner/Agent

_____
Type or print clearly name of owner/agent

_____
Address of owner/agent

#20: Notice of Belief of Abandonment (b)

1. This form initiates the procedure for the owner to recover his real property when the rent has not been paid for 14 days and the owner believes that the renter may not return.

2. The renter is still liable for the unpaid rent until the rental is rerented or until the property is surrendered by the renter.

3. The names of all adult tenants must appear exactly as they do on the rental agreement.

4. Keep one copy for your files and mail one copy to the renter at his last known address and to any other address you might reasonably expect the renter to receive the notice.

5. The property will not be considered abandoned if:

   a. The renter responds in writing of his intent not to abandon the property prior to the time limit.

   b. The renter pays some portion of the past due rent.

   c. The renter can show that the owner did not have reasonable belief the property was abandoned.

   d. The rent was not due and payable for 14 days.

6. If the renter fails to respond within the notice period then at the end of that period the owner may enter the premises and take the neccessary action to rerent the property.

7. The renter may be liable for costs of repair.

8. No rent can be collected from the renter after the date of surrender.

#21: Notice of Right to Reclaim Abandoned Personal Property (Value less than $300.00)

To: _____
          Full Names of All Former Residents

When you vacated the premises:_____,

the following personal property remained: (see below)

   Unless you pay the reasonable cost of storage for all the below described personal

property and take possession of the property which you claim, not later than 18 days after

this notice is deposited in the mail, this personal property may be disposed of according

to state Civil Code Section PDQ

   Because this property is believed to be worth less than $300.00, it may be kept, sold or

destroyed without further notice if you fail to claim it within the time specified below.

Date of mailing of this notice: _____

Date of expiration of this notice: _____

You may claim this property at:

_____

_____
        owner/agent

The abandoned personal property is described as follows:

_____

_____

_____

_____

#22: Notice of Right to Reclaim Abandoned Personal Property (Value more than $300.00) (a)

To: _____

Full Names of All Former Residents

When you vacated the premises:_____,

the following personal property remained: (see below)

Unless you pay the reasonable cost of storage for all the below described personal property and take possession of the property which you claim, not later than 18 days after this notice is deposited in the mail, this personal property may be disposed of according to state Civil Code Section PDQ.

If you fail to reclaim the property, it will be sold at a public sale after notice of the sale has been given by publication. You have the right to bid on the property at this sale. After the property is sold, the cost of storage, advertising, and sale will be deducted and the balance paid to the county. You may claim the balance within one year from that time.

Date of mailing of this notice: _____

Date of expiration of this notice: _____

You may claim this property at:

_____

_____

owner/agent

The abandoned personal property is described as follows:

_____

_____

_____

_____

#22: Notice of Right to Reclaim Abandoned Personal Property (Value more than $300.00) (b)

1. This form provides the rental owner a legal procedure for disposal of personal property believed abandoned by a former resident.

2. Complete the names of all former residents exactly as they appear on your rental agreement. Include the names of any other persons believed to own any of the personal property.

3. List a complete inventory and attach it to the notice.

4. Keep one copy for your files and mail one copy to each person named, at the last known address, and to any other address you might reasonably expect that person to receive the notice.

5. Service may be made by first class mail or by anyone over the age of 18 personally serving the notice.

6. The person believed to be the owner of the personal property can get the property by paying the reasonable costs of storage prior to the end of the notice period.

7. If the resident fails to respond, and the perceived value of the personal property is less than $300.00 the owner may keep it, sell it, or destroy it.

8. If the resident fails to respond and the perceived value of the personal property is more than $300.00 the owner must publish a notice of public sale once a week for two consecutive weeks in a local newspaper of general circulation, giving a description of the personal property and the time and location of the sale.

9. The resident can redeem his personal property up to the date of sale by paying the reasonable storage costs and other expenses.

#22: Notice of Right to Reclaim Abandoned Personal Property (Value more than $300.00) (c)

10. Be sure to make a complete and accurate inventory. Packages, locked suitcases, boxes and so forth need only be described by their outer appearance.

11. Reasonable care should be taken to protect the property.

12. The real property owner is not liable for any losses to the personal property unless he is negligent.

13. If in doubt about the value, get an appraisal.

14. The real property owner may not deduct from the sale proceeds: past due rent, cleaning or damage expenses, other money owed from the resident.

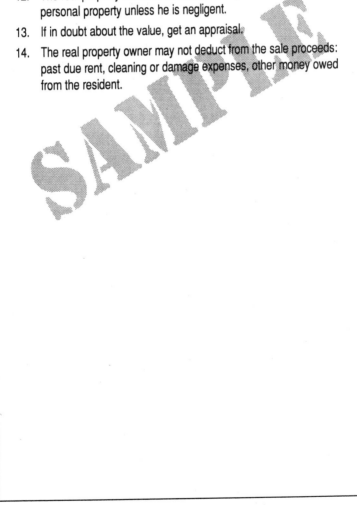

#23: Itemized Disposition of Security Deposit (a)

Pursuant to State Civil Code Section SD, Owner, on _____,

Date

furnished to former resident(s)_____

for the premises located at_____,

the following:

1. Security deposit received:_____

2. Itemized Disposition of Security Deposit:

  A) Itemized Damages:

  _____

  _____

  _____

  _____

  _____

  _____

  _____

          Total Damages: $ _____

  B) Necessary cleaning of premises upon termination:

  _____

  _____

  _____

  _____

  _____

  _____

  _____

          Total Cleaning Costs: $ _____

#23: Itemized Disposition of Security Deposit (b)

C) Past due rent:

_____

_____

_____

_____

_____

_____

_____

_____

_____

Total Rent Due: $ _____

Total Charges $ _____

Balance Due Owner(Please remit immediately) $ _____

Balance Due Resident(Paid by check #_____) $ _____

_____
                                    Owner/Agent

#24: Cleaning Checklist (a)

Kitchen

1. Defrost refrigerator
   a. Wash inside of refrigerator with warm water.
   b. Take out vegetable tray and wash.
   c. Wash and dry outside of refrigerator.
   d. Move refrigerator to clean wall behind it and underneath it.

2. Stove
   a. Remove racks, floor of oven, broiler trays, broiler floor and place on papers laid on counter. Cover with oven cleaner, going by directions on bottle.
   b. Clean inside of oven.
   c. Remove burners and clean, and clean beneath burners where spills and dust may have collected.
   d. Wash and shine stove top, outside of oven, and storage space.

3. Cabinets and drawers and floor
   a. Wash off cupboards, wipe out drawers and shelves, inside and out.
   b. Clean sink and counter top.
   c. Wash kitchen floor and remove all old wax. Then wax with good, clear liquid wax. *Please do not use pastewax!*

4. Miscellaneous in and near kitchen
   a. Wash light fixture.
   b. Take front off air conditioner and clean cover. Wash filter in warm suds in sink, rinse and drain.
   c. Clean fan over stove.
   d. Wash walls and woodwork.
   e. Scrub kitchen chairs with ammonia water.
   f. Wash windows and window tracks.
   g. Scrub patio and wash outside of air conditioner.

#24: Cleaning Checklist(b)

Living room
1. Wash windows inside and out, sills and woodwork, and window tracks.
2. Polish furniture.
3. Clean walls.
4. Wash lamp bowls.
5. Vacuum furniture and floors.
6. Clean shelf and floor of closet.
7. Take heater apart and clean inside and out.
8. Wash traverse rods.

Bedrooms
1. Wash shelf and floor of closet.
2. Clean window and sill and window tracks.
3. Clean walls and woodwork.
4. Clean dresser mirror and wipe out drawers.
5. Wash light fixtures.
6. Wash bed pads.
7. Vacuum bedroom floors and mattress. If tile floor, it must be washed and waxed.

Bathroom
1. Clean bathtub, shower curtains and polish fixtures.
2. Wash toilet inside and out.
3. Clean sink and polish fixtures.
4. Clean inside medicine cabinet and mirror.
5. Wash light fixture.
6. Clean window and window tracks.
7. Wash woodwork, walls, and tile.
8. Wash and wax bathroom floor.

All of this must be done and checked by the owner or manager to insure return of cleaning deposit. No unit will be checked after dark.

#25: Tenant Ledger (payment record)

Tenant Name: Rita Renter   Phone (h) 456-6543
                                                        (w) 456-3210

Rental Address: 4321 Apple St #2
                             Bananaville, CA

Move in date: Rent: $500.00/mo
Move out date: Dep: $750.00

Rental terms: 1 yr lease, No pets, No waterbed

1992	Item	Amt. Pd.	Bal. Due
2/6	Rent (2/10/92 to 3/10/92)	$500.00	
2/6	Deposit	$750.00	
3/2	Rent (3/10 to 4/1)	$334.00	
4/1	Rent (April)	$500.00	
5/2	Rent (May)	$500.00	
6/3	Rent (June)	$500.00	

#26: Repair Record (work order)

To: Phil Phixxit   Date: 5/22/92

From: Ollie Owner

Job Location: 4321 Apple St. #2
                        Bananaville, CA

Phone: 456-6543

Description of work:

                Air conditioner not working, schedule with
                Rita Renter ASAP

Send bill to: Ollie Owner
Date work completed:
Amount due:

#27: Petty-Cash Voucher Envelope

Petty Cash: Banana Apts.

From: 5/1/92 to 6/1/92

Date	Paid To	For	Amount
5/2	Handy Cleaners	Shampoo #5	$35.00
5/2	Stella Sweep	Cleaning #5	$25.00
5/6	Banana Hdwr.	Supplies	$15.25
5/10	Green Ldscp.	Mo. Service	$55.00
5/28	Phixxit	Repair a/c #2	$42.00

Fund Amount:	$200.00	Vouchers Paid:	$172.25
Total pd & cash	$200.00	Cash on hand:	$27.75
Over/Short	$ 0	Total	$200.00

#28: Cash Receipt

Date: 6/3/92   #91

Received from: Rita Renter

Amt: $500.00

For Rent of: 4321 Apple St. #2, Bananaville

Rental Period: 6/1/92   to   7/1/92

Paid by: ___Cash ___Check ___Money Order

Received by: Ollie Owner

SAMPLE

State Consumer Protection Offices

The following is a list of state Consumer Protection Offices. Many are located in governors' or state attorney generals' offices. Check with them for locations of local offices and for state landlord/tenant information.

ALABAMA
Division of Consumer Protection
Attorney General's Office
State House, Room 429
11 S Union Street
Montgomery, AL 36130
205-261-7334

ALASKA
Consumer Protection Section
Attorney General's Office
1031 W 4th Avenue, Suite 110
Anchorage, AK 99501
907-276-3350

ARIZONA
Financial Fraud Division
Office of Attorney General
Department of Law
1275 W Washington Street
Phoenix, AZ 85007
602-542-3702
800-352-8431

ARKANSAS
Consumer Protection/Advocacy Div
Office of Attorney General
200 Tower Building
323 Center Street
Little Rock, AR 72201
501-682-2341

CALIFORNIA
Department of Consumer Affairs
400 R Street
Sacramento, CA 95814
916-445-1591

COLORADO
Consumer Protection Unit
Office of Attorney General
Department of Law
State Services Bldg, Room 215
1525 Sherman Street
Denver, CO 80203
303-866-5168

CONNECTICUT
Department of Consumer Protection
State Office Building, Room 105
165 Capitol Avenue
Hartford, CT 06106
203-566-2559

DELAWARE
Division of Consumer Affairs
Department of Community Affairs
Elbert N Carvel State Office Bldg, 4th fl
820 N French Street
Wilmington, DE 19801
302-571-3250

DISTRICT OF COLUMBIA
Dept of Consumer & Reg Affairs
North Potomac Building, Room 1120
614 H Street, NW
Washington, DC 19801
202-727-7170

FLORIDA
Division of Cons Services, Mayo Bldg
407 S Calhoun Street
Tallahassee, FL 32399-0800
904-488-2226
800-327-3382 (FL)

GEORGIA
Governor's Office of Cons Affairs
2 Martin Luther King, Jr, Dr, SE
Atlanta, GA 30334
404-656-1760

HAWAII
Office of Consumer Protection
Dept of Commerce & Cons Affairs
James Campbell Estate Building
826 Fort Street Mall, Suite 600B
PO Box 3767
Honolulu HI, 96813
808-548-2560

IDAHO
Attorney General
State Capitol Building, Room 210
700 W Jefferson Street
Boise, ID 83270
208-334-2400

ILLINOIS
Southern Region
Consumer Protection Division
Office of Attorney General
500 S 2nd Street
Springfield, IL 62706
217-782-9011

Northern Region
Consumer Protection Division
Office of Attorney General
State of Illinois Center, 13th floor
100 W Randolph Street
Chicago, IL 60601
312-917-3580

INDIANA
Consumer Protection Division
Office of Attorney General
State House, Room 219
200 W Washington Street
Indianapolis, IN 46204
317-232-6330

IOWA
Consumer Protection Division
Office of Attorney General
Hoover State Office Building
1300 E Walnut Street
Des Moines, IA 50319
525-281-5926

KANSAS
Consumer Protection Division
Office of Attorney General
Kansas Judicial Center Building, 2nd floor
301 W 10th Street
Topeka, KS 66612
913-296-3751

KENTUCKY
Division of Consumer Protection
Office of Attorney General
Executive Building
209 St. Clair Street
Frankfort, KY 40601-1875
502-342-7013

LOUISIANA
Consumer Protection Section
Office of Attorney General
Department of Justice
PO Box 94005, Capitol Station
Baton Rouge, LA 70804
504-342-7013

MAINE
Bureau of Consumer Credit Protection
Dept of Prof & Financial Regulation
Hallowell, ME 04347
207-582-8718
Mail to: State House, Station 35
Augusta, ME 04333

MARYLAND
Consumer Protection Division
Office of Attorney General
Munsey Building
7 N Calvert Street
Baltimore, MD 21202
301-528-8662

MASSACHUSETTS
Exec Office of Cons Affairs & Bus Reg
John W McCormack State Office Bldg
Rm 1411
One Ashburton Place
Boston, MA 02108
617-727-7755

MICHIGAN
Consumers Council
Hollister Building, Room 414
106 W Allegan Street
Lansing, MI 48933
517-373-0701

MINNESOTA
Consumer Division
Office of Attorney General
Ford Building, Room 200
117 University Ave
St. Paul, MN 55155
612-296-3353

MISSISSIPPI
Bureau of Regulatory Services
Department of Agriculture & Commerce
Walter Sillers State Office Bldg, Rm 1602
550 High Street
Mail to: PO Box 1609
Jackson, MS 39215-1609
601-359-3636

MISSOURI
Consumer Protection Division
Office of Attorney General
Supreme Court Building
Mail to: PO Box 899
Jefferson City, MO 65102
314-751-3321

MONTANA
Consumer Affairs Unit
Department of Commerce
1424 9th Avenue
Helena, MT 59620-0420
406-444-4312

NEBRASKA
Consumer Affairs Division
Office of Attorney General
Department of Justice
State Capitol, Room 2115
Lincoln, NE 68509
402-471-4723

NEVADA
Consumer Affairs Division
Department of Commerce
2601 E Sahara Avenue, Suite 247
Las Vegas, NV 89104
702-885-4340

NEW HAMPSHIRE
Cons Protection & Antitrust Bureau
Office of Attorney General
State House Annex, Room 308
25 Capitol Street
Concord, NH 03301
603-271-3641

NEW JERSEY
Division of Consumer Affairs
Department of Law & Public Safety
1100 Raymond Blvd, Room 504
Newark, NJ 07102
201-648-4010

NEW MEXICO
Cons Protection & Economic Crimes Div
Office of Attorney General
Bataan Memorial Building
Mail to: PO Drawer 1508
Santa Fe, NM 87504-1508

NEW YORK
Consumer Protection Board
Executive Department
99 Washington Ave, Room 1020
Albany, NY 12210
518-474-2257

NORTH CAROLINA
Cons Protection & Antitrust Section
Department of Justice
104 Fayetteville Street
Raleigh, NC 27602
919-733-7741

NORTH DAKOTA
Consumer Fraud & Antitrust Division
Office of Attorney General
State Capitol
Bismarck, ND 58505
701-224-3404

OHIO
Consumer Protection Division
Office of Attorney General
State Office Tower
30 E Broad Street
Columbus, OH 43266-0410
614-466-8831

OKLAHOMA
Department of Consumer Credit
Jim Thorpe Office Bldg, Ste 104
4545 Lincoln Boulevard
Oklahoma City, OK 73105
405-521-3653

OREGON
Civil Enforcement Division
Department of Justice
100 Justice Building
Portland, OR 97310
503-378-4732

PENNSYLVANIA
Bureau of Consumer Protection
Office of Attorney General
Strawberry Square Bldg, 14th Fl.
4th & Walnut Streets
Harrisburg, PA 17120
717-787-9707

RHODE ISLAND
Consumer's Council
365 Broadway
Providence, RI 02909
401-277-2764

SOUTH CAROLINA
Department of Consumer Affairs
Carolina Continental Insurance Building
2nd floor
2801 Devine Street
Columbia, SC 29250-5757
803-734-9458
800-922-1594 (SC)

SOUTH DAKOTA
Division of Consumer Affairs
Office of Attorney General
Capitol Building
500 E Capitol Avenue
Pierre, SD 57501
605-773-4400

TENNESSEE
Division of Consumer Affairs
500 James Robertson Parkway, 5th floor
Nashville, TN 37219
615-741-4737
800-342-8385 (TN)

TEXAS
Consumer Protection Division
Office of Attorney General
American Legion Building
15th Street & Congress Avenue
Austin, TX 78711
512-463-2070

UTAH
Consumer Protection Division
Department of Business Regulation
Heber W Wells Building, 4th floor
160 East, 300 South
Salt Lake City, UT 84145-0801
801-530-6601

VERMONT
Public Protection Division
Office of Attorney General
Pavillion Office Building
109 State Street
Montpelier, VT 05602
802-828-3171

VIRGINIA
State Office of Consumer Affairs
Dept of Agriculture & Consumer Services
Washington Building-Capitol Square
1100 Bank Street
Richmond, VA 23209
804-786-2042
800-552-9963 (VA)

WASHINGTON
Attorney General's Office
Consumer & Business Fair Practices
    Division
Department of Consumer Protection
Highways-Licenses Building, 7th floor
12th & Franklin
Olympia, WA 98504
206-586-2563
800-551-4636

WEST VIRGINIA
Consumer Protection Division
Office of Attorney General
812 Quarrier Street
Charleston, WV 25301
304-8986
800-368-8808 (WV)

WISCONSIN
Trade & Consumer Protection Division
Department of Agriculture, Trade &
    Consumer Protection
801 W Badger Road
Madison, WI 53708
608-266-7220

WYOMING
Consumer Affairs Division
Office of Attorney General
State Capitol, Room 123
200 W 24th Street
Cheyenne, WY 82002
307-777-6286

PUERTO RICO
Department of Consumer Affairs
Minillas Government Center, North
    Building
5th floor
De Diego Avenue
Santurce, PR 00940
809-721-3280

VIRGIN ISLANDS
Department of Licensing & Consumer
    Affairs
St Thomas, VI 00801
809-774-3130

Index